RECOLLECTIONS

OF

SEVENTY YEARS

By

Mrs. John Farrar

Boston
Ticknor and Fields

1865

PREFACE.

IT has often been proposed to me to write the history of my life, by friends who have listened with pleasure to many narratives connected with it; but I have not been convinced that the strictly personal part of my history has anything in it worth laying before the public.

Conscious, however, of having been acquainted with many remarkable characters, and holding in my memory not a few unwritten romances, I have consented to put on paper some of those past experiences, hoping that the Recollections of Seventy Years of varied life may have the same interest for my readers that my oral narratives have had for my auditors.

Mine are "plain, unvarnished tales," never exaggerated, never embellished. Every anecdote depends for its value on its perfect truth; and as most of them belong to my life in the Old World, and to persons who are no longer living, I trust that no one's feelings will be hurt by my disclosures. I have in a few instances suppressed names, or given fictitious ones.

CONTENTS.

PAGE

INTRODUCTION 1

CHAPTER

I. RESIDENCE. — SIEGE OF DUNKIRK. — FRENCH REVOLUTION. — DÉTENUS 7

II. ROBESPIERRE. — DEPARTURE FOR ENGLAND. — ABBÉ GRÉGOIRE 17

III. MRS. BARBAULD. — MR. AND MRS. OPIE. — BENJAMIN WEST. — GEORGE THE THIRD. — MRS. KNOWLES 23

IV. ELIZABETH FRY 33

V. MILFORD HAVEN. — FRENCH SPY. — FRENCH AT FISHGUARD 38

VI. LADY HAMILTON. — LORD NELSON. — CASTLE HALL AND ITS COMPANY 47

VII. HERBERT FAMILY. — SAILOR-BOY. — WANDERING GIRL. — ORLEANS FAMILY 56

VIII. CRABBE. — BUXTON. — JOANNA BAILLIE . . 67

IX. LADY MACWORTH 76

X. PRINCESS CARABOO 83

XI. THE ENGLISH STAGE. — MRS. JORDAN 92

XII. BATH. — BEAU NASH. — THE B——— FAMILY . 97

XIII. IRELAND. — SIR HARRY BROWN HAYES. — BRENAN 107

XIV. MISS EDGEWORTH 118

XV. ANDRIANE 128

XVI. THE FRENCH STAGE 133

XVII. MR. AND MRS. THOMAS HOPE 140

XVIII. The Misses Allen. — Mrs. Sismondi. — The Young Widow 146
XIX. Lady Mansfield. — Children in a Cave. — The Haunted House 153
XX. Mariages de Convenance 163
XXI. Unhappy Marriages 171
XXII. Greenwich Observatory. — Mrs. Somerville. — Dr. Robinson. — Observatory at Armagh 184
XXIII. A Remarkable Woman 195
XXIV. Princess Charlotte 202
XXV. Hannah More's Convert 219
XXVI. A Converted Jew 231
XXVII. Edinburgh 236
XXVIII. Salt Mines 241
XXIX. Novello Family 248
XXX. Voyages 255
XXXI. Switzerland 265
XXXII. A Travelling Companion . . . 273
XXXIII. Weariness of Etiquette 278
XXXIV. The Maid of Honor. — The Orphans. — The General's Lady 283
XXXV. Parental Authority 291
XXXVI. The Village Apothecary 295
XXXVII. The Gardener's Granddaughter . . 298
XXXVIII. Lunatic Asylums 306
XXXIX. Courts of Law 314
XL. Miss Delia Bacon 319

INTRODUCTION.

IN order to give some coherence to my various narratives, it seems necessary to describe their whereabouts, and my connection with them. As my earliest recollections date back to the time when my parents and grand-parents were residing in Dunkirk, during the latter part of the reign of Louis XVI., I will begin with giving a short account of my grandfather's establishing the whale-fishery in France.

William Rotch was a native of Nantucket, and a member of the Society of Friends. Most of the inhabitants of that island were of that sect, and, professing peace principles, they endeavored to preserve a strict neutrality during the Revolutionary War. The consequence of this was, that they were made the prey of both parties, and my grandfather was often deputed to carry their grievances before the Provisional Government of the Colony, and also to the head-quarters of the British commanders. This was a service of great danger, and his life was often in jeopardy; but his courage and presence of mind were always equal to the occasion, and he saved the island from utter devastation, though not from heavy losses of property. Two hundred vessels were captured by the English, and he lost to the amount of sixty thousand dollars. In one night the boats of a man-of-war, commanded by midshipmen, landed their crews on Nantucket, and burnt ten thousand dollars' worth of oil for my grandfather, besides destroying the property of others.

At the close of the war, when peace and independence had been conquered, the inhabitants of Nantucket found themselves in a ruinous condition; their commerce and their fishery were destroyed, and many left the island to seek their fortunes on the mainland; others preferred to continue in the whale-fishery if they could find a place where it could be pursued to advantage. Before the separation from the mother country, they had there found a market for all the oil they could catch; but the duty was now made so heavy, that it would not pay to send oil to England. The distresses of these once prosperous islanders determined my grandfather to go to England, and endeavor to interest that government in their condition, as Quakers, who from peace principles had never taken up arms against the mother country, and who would be willing to emigrate to England, and carry on from there the whale-fishery, provided they were aided by British money, and allowed to bring with them, free of duty, their oil and their ships. Deeply interested in this enterprise, he embarked for England on board a vessel of his own, named the Maria, and I have often heard the old gentleman tell with pride and pleasure, that she was the first ship that ever unfurled the flag of the United States in the Thames.

William Rotch was a very handsome man, tall and erect, dressed in a whole suit of light drab broadcloth, with knee-breeches, shoes, and buckles; his head was a little bald, with flowing white locks, while still in the prime of life. His appearance commanded respect, and his manners were as polite as Quaker sincerity would permit. Arrived in London, he soon made his way to the presence of the Chancellor of the Exchequer, Mr. Pitt, who listened patiently to his account of the disasters which had befallen his native island, in consequence of the war and the peace principles of its inhabitants. When he urged their claims on the British government, Mr. Pitt said, "Undoubtedly you are right, sir; what can we do for you?" Mr. Rotch then told him that a number of families were willing to remove to England and to carry on the whale-fishery, if sufficiently aided and encouraged to do so. Here the conversation ended, and the subject was laid before the Privy Council. The secretary, Mr. Cotterel, sent a note to my grandfather, saying, the Council would sit on an early day, when they would hear what he had to offer. He waited a whole month for that "early day," and then applied to the secretary to know the reason of the delay. He pleaded their having so much business before them that they had not been able to attend to his; and with this excuse, they kept the American Quaker waiting four months. Then he requested to have a person appointed to confer with him. Unhappily, Lord Hawkesbury was the man fixed upon, and a greater enemy of the United States could not have been found. After several unsatisfactory and very disagreeable interviews, Mr. Rotch refused all further negotiation, and told him that he should carry his proposals to France.

Lord Hawkesbury did not relish the idea of France having the benefit of such a nursery for seamen as the whale-fishery would give them, and he tried hard to bend the Quaker to his purpose, but in vain. He and his son left London immediately, and proceeded in the Maria to Dunkirk, whence they sent their proposals to the French government, and were summoned to appear in Paris. There they were treated with marked attention, and whilst their peculiarities of dress, speech, and manners excited wonder and curiosity, their scruples were always respected. Every privilege which they asked for was freely granted, so important was it considered to have the whale-fishery established in France.

The Nantucketers settled in Dunkirk were to have the right to bring over their ships loaded with oil, the ships to be registered as French vessels, and the oil to be admitted duty free. All the officers to be employed on board of whalers were to be Americans, and bounties were to be given by the government for every full cargo brought home. In return for these privileges, each vessel was to have on board a certain number of young landsmen bound as apprentices to the owner, and these were to be made good seamen.

That once flourishing town of Dunkirk had lost its commerce, and grass was growing in its once busy streets; but it appeared to my grandfather very eligible for his purposes, and so it proved. He returned home with his son, to make the necessary preparations for his grand undertaking. My father's chief preparation was getting married, and as it required much time then to build vessels and catch oil enough to fill them, he became a householder, and a father, before he went to France to live.

When he did set sail for Dunkirk with his wife, he was obliged, by her extreme sea-sickness, to put back, after being out ten days. It seemed necessary, to save her life, and he was obliged to proceed alone on his important enterprise, and, as the partner of his father and brothers, he established the whale-fishery in France.

Sarah L. Watson,

RECOLLECTIONS OF SEVENTY YEARS.

CHAPTER I.

RESIDENCE. — SIEGE OF DUNKIRK. — FRENCH REVOLUTION. — DÉTENUS.

WHEN at last my father was established in Dunkirk, the outfit of his whaling ships was the revival of trade in that town, and the inhabitants welcomed the strangers who brought them wealth and prosperity. As the crews and the officers of the whaling ships were from Nantucket, and some of these had their families with them, there was a large number of Americans in Dunkirk. Many English also were attracted thither by the brisk business created by the fishery.

After a separation of two years, my mother resolved, even at the risk of her life, to join her husband in Dunkirk, and his parents and sisters went with her, all strict Quakers, and objects of curiosity to the French, who saw for the first time the peculiarities of that sect, and could not understand either their faith or their scruples.

The residence in a French town of such an exemplary family of Friends, was hailed by the English Quakers as affording an excellent opportunity for promulgating their doctrines, and a succession of preachers came over to Dunkirk for that purpose, and always stayed at our house. As they spake no French, my father used to act as their interpreter, but once, when he could not attend, a person was employed in his stead. The preacher began his discourse with these words, "Job was an upright man"; and they were rendered into a French expression equivalent to "Job was a tall, gentlemanly man," and the rest of the sermon was, probably, no nearer than that to the real meaning.

The peace principles of the Quakers will not allow of any demonstration of pleasure at a victory won by force of arms, in any cause, and when the whole town was in a ferment of joy for the success of the French arms, and was making great preparations for a general illumination, these conscientious Quakers refused to illuminate. The Mayor of Dunkirk was a good friend of my father, and urged him to do it as a mere act of self-preservation, "for," said he, "the people will be so exasperated by your not illuminating, that they will commit some outrageous act of violence, from which I cannot protect you." Fully aware of the danger they would incur, both father and son were resolved, in spite of all the remonstrances of their friends, not to illuminate; they would maintain their principles at all hazards.

When their neighbors were lighting up their houses, they shut their shutters, locked and barred their doors, and retired to a back parlor, to await their fate. It was a very solemn time for them all, and was spent in silent prayer. At the end of an hour, the door-bell rang, and my father chose to answer it, though he expected, on opening it, to be assailed by an angry mob. Instead of this, a friend entered, exclaiming, "I am glad to see that you have illuminated after all." "But I have not done it." "Yes, your house is illuminated, and very prettily done too." In utter amazement my father went into the street, and saw a large frame-work of wood covered with lights, and put up against the front of the house. This was the work of the Mayor to save the good Quakers from destruction.

Though the French could not comprehend the principles of these strange people, they honored them for their adherence to them, and always bore kindly with their peculiarities. Even when the town of Dunkirk was besieged by the English, and all citizens who could bear arms turned out to defend their homes from the invader, my father was excused from the duty of a soldier, and appointed commander of the fire department, a post of danger which he solicited. The firing of hot shot sometimes produced a conflagration, and *that spot* became the point toward which the enemy directed their guns. It was, of course, a dangerous place to those engaged in extinguishing the fire. My father thus proved that it was not cowardice that prevented his taking up arms.

I will now describe that siege of Dunkirk, as I have heard my father relate it.

One of the numerous acts of the British government to destroy the Revolutionary power in France, was sending a large force, under the command of the Duke of York, son of George III., to besiege and take the city of Dunkirk. He sat down before the town in the most approved manner of those times. The wide plain beyond the city was covered with the tents of the English army, while rows of cannon and mortars seemed to threaten the ancient walls of Dunkirk with certain destruction. The peaceful inhabitants were much alarmed, and every citizen capable of bearing arms was enrolled as a soldier; for there was no military force there, and the English might have marched into the town and taken it at once; but not knowing its defenceless state, they began to bombard it with hot and cold shot. Orders were given by the

Mayor that there should be in every room of every house a pail of water and a pair of tongs, to pick up and quench the hot shot; also, every closet door must stand open, and all the women and children were advised to leave the town. All those who could afford it went off to Calais and put up at Dessein's famous hotel. They rushed off in such haste as to be very ill provided with clothes, and some days after that, when my mother and her children arrived with ample wardrobes, her clothes were borrowed by all her friends, and as she wore the Quaker costume, she was amused to see her plain garments on gay, fashionable Frenchwomen.

A courier arrived daily from Dunkirk and proclaimed, from the steps of the Town Hall, the progress of the siege. All the fugitive ladies would run out, without bonnet or shawl, and stand around him to hear the news. There came letters from their husbands written without any regard to truth, merely to suit the wishes of the writer. If a man had a very timid wife, and was fearful she would fly farther, he would tell her that the town was very quiet, and he was in no danger. If a husband was afraid his wife would return inopportunely, he would write that the enemy was at the gates of the city, half of its inhabitants were killed, and the streets ran blood. These ladies, living together, naturally compared the accounts they received, and finding them so very contradictory, they knew not what to believe ; some were very angry, and all were much annoyed. At last one of them said, let us ask Madame Rotch what her husband writes, for the Quakers do not lie. They did so, heard the truth, and ever after relied on her letters for their news of the siege.

A force sufficient to defend the town was soon sent to Dunkirk, and some little fighting took place without the walls, but the cannonading of the town did little damage. The merchants used to dine round at each other's houses, eat up all their wives' preserves and other good things, and have a jolly time of it. One morning the cannonading did not begin as early as usual, and, on looking through their telescopes, the men on the ramparts could see no movement in the British camp. At last the truth dawned on them, that the English had run away in the night. A visit to the camp showed with what haste they had departed. In the Duke of York's tent were found his watch and all his dressing equipage. This extraordinary retreat excited the utmost contempt of the French, and the indignation of the English people. The Duke of York was deprived of his command, and it was several years before he was again employed.

I have hitherto related only what I remember to have heard from others; but now I come to a period when I can remember what I saw myself, and it is not wonderful that, living in the midst of a bloody revolution, my earliest recollection should be the sight of the *guillotine*, erected in the great square of the town of Dunkirk. Sent out to walk before breakfast, with my nurse, we happened to see it just arrived, and in the process of erection. On my return home I told my mother of it, with childish glee, and was astonished at the horror with which she heard my account.

At this time the Revolutionary government decreed that all the British subjects then in France should be imprisoned, and my nurse, being an Englishwoman, was shut up in a nunnery, used as a prison, after the nuns had been liberated. It was in vain to tell her that her life was not in danger; she was extremely frightened, and to calm her fears and make her imprisonment less tedious, my mother sent me every morning to pass several hours with her; so visits to a nun's cell are among my earliest recollections. My mother valued relics so much, that she sent a good chair of her own to be exchanged for the shabby old one of the cell occupied by my nurse, and I have that nun's chair now.

After the imprisonment of the English in France, two American ladies were walking on the ramparts of Dunkirk and conversing together. A sentinel said to his comrade, "All the English are not in prison; shall we arrest those?" On hearing this, one of the speakers said to the soldier, "We are Americans, and we speak the American language." Both the men applauded them, for the French loved America in those days.

Another instance of female courage occurs to my mind as happening in that same town of Dunkirk. Mrs. R., an American lady, was conversing with a gentleman who had some care of her during the absence of her husband in Paris. It was after nine o'clock, and he was preparing to go home, when a servant stole quietly into the room, and whispered to her mistress, that the man-servant had brought two armed men into the house; they were now in his room, and she had no doubt that they would rob the house and murder the family. Mrs. R. tried to allay her fears, by saying those men were probably friends of Joseph, and were merely paying him a visit, and she desired the girl to keep quiet in the kitchen and she would send the soldiers away. Her friend Captain M. offered to speak to the men for her, but she thought it best to try first if she could manage them, and keep the Captain for a reserve force; so she went to the foot of the stairs, leading up from the kitchen to the man's room, and said, "Joseph, it is time for your friends to go home, and for you to shut up the house and go to bed; send them away directly." Joseph made no reply, and she returned to the parlor to wait the effect of her commands. They availed nothing, so she went again, in spite of Captain M's. remonstrance and wish to go himself. Her objection to his going was, that it would appear as if she was alarmed, and she meant that her authority, as mistress of the house, should prevail.

She told Joseph those men must come down and leave her house directly, and added, "If they do not move at once, I will come up to them." One would suppose that armed men would laugh at such a vain threat, but so far from it, they obeyed at once. To get out of the house they had to pass by the open parlor door, and Mrs. R. placed herself so as to see them pass through an entry in which stood a rocking-horse with a child's hat hung on his head. One of the men seized the hat and was carrying it off, when she called to him to let that hat alone, and he threw it back into the entry. "Well done!" said the Captain, "you are a brave woman. I should have let him carry off the hat."

Among the English *détenus*, as they were called, was the author and poet, Helen Maria Williams, well known in this country as the writer of that beautiful hymn, beginning, "While Thee I seek, protecting Power." She was acquainted with my father, and hearing that he was in Paris, when she was imprisoned, she sent for him, and begged him, as an American, to claim her as his wife and so procure her liberty. The truthful Quaker was not so corrupted by his residence in France, as to be willing to make this false claim; he was, however, induced by her eloquent pleading, to promise not to deny what she might say on the subject, unless directly questioned. She succeeded in obtaining her liberty and fled to England. The apparent indifference of the supposed husband threw no discredit on her pretended relation to him.

ROBESPIERRE. — DEPARTURE FOR ENGLAND. — ABBÉ GRÉGOIRE.

I HAVE so often heard my father describe Robespierre that I feel as I had myself seen that mean-looking, little man, with his ruffles, and his hair elaborately dressed. As it was considered, in those days, that to be well dressed was anti-republican, his elaborate toilet was the more remarkable. My father narrowly escaped with his life, after an interview with this worst of tyrants. He was deputed by the American merchants of Dunkirk, who were suffering under an act of embargo, to take up a petition for its removal from vessels belonging to so friendly a power as the United States. He was to read the petition at the bar of the National Convention; a body of men who were supposed to represent the will of the people, but were, at that time, entirely subservient to the will of one man, and that man Robespierre. He allowed the House to appoint only one committee, called the Committee of Public Safety; to that all important cases were referred, and there Robespierre ruled every decision. Over the door of the committee-room was written, "Engrossed by the affairs of the nation, we have no time to consider private claims."

My father was told that he must read his petition to Robespierre, before he attempted to read it in the National Convention; so he sought an interview with that dangerous man at his own residence. He was shown through a suite of shabby rooms, where the family were employed in household work, to a long, unfurnished hall, where he found half a dozen gentlemen waiting to see the despot. There was not a seat in the room, until a door opened and Robespierre entered, in his dressing-gown, followed by his hair-dresser, who carried a chair in his hand for his master to sit on whilst he was powdered. When powder was generally worn, it was the custom to put it on, in some small room or closet devoted to the purpose, and to powder in the presence of another person was considered an insult. That Robespierre should come into his audience-chamber to perform that part of his toilet was a piece of arrogance and rudeness never to be forgotten. The hair-dresser applied the powder-puff until there was a cloud of powder all around him, and of course the dark coats, in waiting, were none the better for it. When the hair-dresser retired, he carried off the chair with him, and Robespierre went up to a mirror and adjusted every hair around his face. He then exchanged his dressing-gown for a coat which his valet brought, and assisted him to put on. That done, he turned to the knot of gentlemen who were standing at one end of the room, and said he was ready to hear what they had to say. Those who spoke before my father did were very summarily disposed of with negative answers. Then he produced his petition, and asked Robespierre to read it. He did so, and returned it, saying, "That petition cannot be presented to the National Convention, for it contains *views to change* the government." Such words from such a man were equivalent to a sentence of death. My father knew it, and perceived at once what was the objectionable part. The merchants asked for a committee to be appointed to examine the claims of American ship-owners, and Robespierre had abolished all committees but the one of which he was the moving power. With wonderful presence of mind my father took out his pencil, struck out that request and showed the paper to Robespierre, who, on seeing the alteration, said *that* might be read the next day at the bar of the National Convention. As my father left the hall, a friend who had accompanied him there, said, "We are a head shorter for this." "Never mind," was the reply, "we shall go in good company."

While my father was reading the petition, Robespierre entered one of the galleries, and as soon as it was ended, he moved that it should be referred to the Committee of Public Safety. This quashed it at once, but the reader's life was saved.

Not until after the fall of Robespierre, was my father permitted to leave France; then he embarked with his whole family and all his valuables on board one of his own vessels, and sailed for America. He was aware that a number of persons had secreted themselves on board his ship, in order to escape from France, and as two custom-house officers accompanied the vessel down the harbor, my father was afraid they would discover the fugitives. To prevent this he provided a handsome lunch and plenty of good wine, of which they partook so largely that they forgot to examine the vessel, and left her in high good humor.

Instead of proceeding to the United States, we landed in England, and our arrival was impressed on my memory by my being checked in singing the following words: —

> " Le Duc de York est un poltron,
> Vive le son, vive le son."

I was told that I was now in the country of the Duke, and must never sing that again. This was unnecessary caution; but we had come from a land where every word must be guarded, lest life should be the forfeit, and it was difficult for us to realize that there was liberty of speech in England.

A suit in chancery to recover the insurance on a vessel burnt at sea, was what took my father to England, and its long duration caused him to settle in that country.

The Abbé Grégoire lived in the time of the first French Revolution. He was a republican in his principles, but a lover of law and order. He was made a Bishop in the Roman Church, but was very liberal in his opinions. My father was on intimate terms with him, and ventured to ask him whether he believed in all the ceremonies of his Church; he said he did not, but added, "We must make religion thick enough for the people to feel it, or it will slip through their fingers."

A better saying of his was one that saved his life. Paris in those days was lighted by glass lanterns called *réverbères*, suspended by ropes over the centre of the street, and the mob were often pleased to use that arrangement for hanging any one obnoxious to them. At one time, every well-dressed man was in danger of this summary punishment, and the Abbé Grégoire being one day too neat and clean to suit the taste of a mob of ruffians, they called him an aristocrat, and cried out, *À la lanterne!* They would have hanged him on the spot, if he had not saved his life by this impromptu *jeu d'esprit:* —

> "Croyez vous voir plus clair,
> Quand je prends la place du réverbere."

The mob applauded him, and he passed on in safety. Courage and presence of mind were much needed in those times.

I remember hearing my father say that he was in Paris when the Queen was beheaded, and that he dared not go out of his hotel before the execution, for fear of seeing some part of it; nor after it was over, for fear his countenance should betray his horror of the deed, and cause his arrest as a loyalist. It happened to my father, more than once, to be engaged to dine with a friend, and when he went to the house, to be told by the servant that his master had been taken the night before to the Conciergerie. Few ever left that prison but to go to execution. It was considered as the next step to the guillotine.

CHAPTER III.

MRS. BARBAULD. — MR. AND MRS. OPIE. — BENJAMIN WEST. — GEORGE THE THIRD. — MRS. KNOWLES.

DICKENS has shown us the great influence which a chancery suit may exert over the lives and characters of all concerned in it. My father's suit continued so many years, that it broke up all his plans of returning to his native land, and planted him for life in England with all the privileges of a British subject. We resided for a time at Islington, a suburb of London, and there my mother made the acquaintance of Mrs. Barbauld, who was then writing for the benefit of her little nephew, Charles Aikin, those hymns and lessons which have since delighted so many children, both in the Old and the New World. Melancholy, however, were the consequences of her devotion to that bright little boy. His brain was overtaxed, and the precocious child became an idiot before he reached maturity.

I remember sitting on Mrs. Barbauld's lap and her asking me if I could read, and what book I was then reading; I answered, "Barbauld's Lessons," quite unconscious that I was sitting in the lap of their author. She then said, "I suppose you study geography, and can tell me what ocean is between England and America." I said, "The Atlantic," which I knew from hearing my mother speak of her relations as being on the other side of the Atlantic, not from any study of geography; and fearing I might not be able to answer another question, I hurried away from her.

I often met her after I was grown up, and remember her as a sweet-looking, lively old lady, wearing her gray hair, which was then very uncommon, and reading aloud to a circle of young people, on a rainy morning in the country. She read well; the book was "Guy Mannering," then just published. When she had given us the description of Meg Merrilies, she asked us all to draw the Gypsy as we imagined her, and very different were the sketches we made. My sister's was the best, but the kind old lady took possession of them all as valuable to her.

Mrs. Opie, another author and poet, as different as possible from Mrs. Barbauld, was an acquaintance of my mother. Her novels were at this time very popular, and her husband was equally famous as an historical painter. He had many admirers, but his works were not of a high order. He made all his male faces with large, ugly noses, so that one could always know his pictures by that feature. My mother had such an instinctive appreciation of painting, that Mr. West made a point of going with her to the annual exhibition of the works of living artists, that he might hear her natural remarks on the principal pictures. She criticised all Opie's so severely that Mr. West feared she might be overheard by him and hastened to tell her whose they were. Mr. West's pictures did not wholly escape her criticism, but she generally knew beforehand which were his.

When Mrs. Opie became a gay widow, we often met her at the house of a mutual friend, where her eccentric conduct amused some, and disgusted others. I have seen her astonish a grave circle of elderly people by jumping up and dancing a shawl-dance then in vogue on the stage, flourishing away to a tune of her own singing, apparently unconscious of the effect she was producing. She used to carry about with her in all her visits a pretty little stringed instrument, in the classic form of a lyre, and sing her own songs, with great expression, to that accompaniment. She said she could always find out the secrets of a young girl's heart, if she could sing to her alone. She tried her experiment on me and proved right.

Mrs. Opie was fair, with delicate features and a form of symmetrical beauty. The well-formed hands and arms were always on exhibition, and short and scanty skirts disclosed the prettiest feet and ankles. Her talents and accomplishments, her novels, her poetry, and her singing, made her, for a time, a favorite with the fashionables of London, and she highly enjoyed her popularity; but it did not last long, and when it failed, she took refuge from the gay world in a circle of wealthy and highly cultivated Quakers. The Gurneys, Barclays, Hoares, Woods, and Frys, were her intimate friends, and after several years passed among them, she joined the Society of Friends and adopted their dress and language. I saw her once after her metamorphosis, and could but remark the discrepancy between her costume and her manners, which still savored of the wicked world. The pretty foot was still seen, though the dress was long and ample, and the glove was unnecessarily taken off to show the beautiful hand. Amelia Opie was not changed, only acting a new part.

I have already mentioned Benjamin West. He was historical painter to George III., but still a true son of America, and much known to Americans in London. My parents were intimate with him, and he always took an interest in their children. My father showed him some flowers of my painting, on which he said, "Do not let her waste her time on such things as these; make her draw heads; any one who can draw or paint the human face divine, will find all other objects easy work." Mrs. West had a very beautiful little spaniel of King Charles's breed, and on my mother's admiring it, Mr. West made a portrait of it for her.

My parents refused to be presented at the Court of St. James, and yet had a great desire to see the Royal family; so Mr. West promised to obtain permission for them to be present in Somerset House, when the Royal family visited the exhibition of pictures there, previous to its being opened to the public. Mr. West always attended the King, on these occasions, to point out to his Majesty the pictures most worthy of his attention, and was always invited to breakfast with him on the morning that he went to Somerset House. During the breakfast, Mr. West obtained leave to admit his Quaker friends to the hall of entrance, and an order was despatched to the guards on duty there to admit us. The commanding officer was very civil and placed us so as to see the royal party to the best advantage.

The King came first, then the Queen, followed by four princesses, and they courteously delayed their passage through the hall for our gratification. Princess Elizabeth said, loud enough for us to hear, that she admired the Quaker bonnet, and should like to wear one, a great stretch of politeness, we thought. The King asked Mr. West if the little girl were a Quaker; I had on a straw bonnet. On hearing that I was, he said, "Tell her that if she had had on a Quaker bonnet I would have spoken to her."

George III. had great fondness for Quakers, and removed some of their restrictions and disabilities. Their marriages were not legal until they were made so in his reign. The reason for his partiality was little known; but I have heard it accounted for thus. When he was a young man, he had a Quaker mistress, to whom he was long faithful. She died just before his marriage, and when his courtiers supposed him to be sleeping quietly in his palace, the night before his marriage, he was travelling *incog.* many miles out of London, to take a last leave of his dying mistress.

George III. was a stout, thick-set man, with a short neck and a red face. He wore a brown wig and a long frock-coat, and without the star on his breast he would have passed for a country squire. The Queen and princesses were all such common-looking people that they upset my childish notions of royalty. I have since learned that all that family were coarse, sensual, and vulgar. George III. did all he could to keep the morals of his daughters pure, but he failed entirely, notwithstanding his strict discipline and constant vigilance. His last attack of insanity, from which he never recovered, was brought on by an interview with the Princess Amelia, on her death-bed, when she confessed to him her marriage, and besought him to be kind to her husband. She was the best of his daughters and the most beloved by him, and as her marriage was not a legal one, the King was greatly shocked by the disclosure.

While living at Islington, we had frequent visits from the learned and accomplished Mrs. Knowles. She was the widow of a physician, who had left her a handsome fortune. She was a member of the Society of Friends, and, when a young woman, had an animated discussion concerning the peculiar tenets of her sect with the dogmatic Dr. Johnson. Their encounter must have been like lightning and thunder, her lively and brilliant remarks followed by the roar of denunciation from the Doctor. Her daring to differ from him, and support her opinions by argument, made her notorious among his admirers and his enemies. Her father had given her the education of a boy, rather than of a girl of those days. She was a good Greek and Latin scholar; but her learning did not prevent her spending most of her time, after marriage, in painting and worsted work. Her manner of doing the latter was peculiar to herself, and produced so fine an effect, that she became famous for it, and was invited to St. James's Palace to show her work to the Royal family. While there, she expressed a strong desire to make a portrait in worsted work of the King, and he very good-naturedly consented to sit for it, little supposing how long it would take ; but her powers of conversation were so great, that he declared he never lost his patience and was well amused all the time.

The likeness proved good, and the Queen claimed it for her own, intending to make Mrs. Knowles a suitable present in return. As she wore a Quaker dress, jewelry would not be acceptable. A piece of plate might be the right thing, but still the Queen was at a loss what to choose ; so she bade one of the gentlemen in waiting to speak with Mrs. Knowles and ascertain what she would prefer. He did so, and she, being very miserly, said she preferred a sum of money.

When the Queen heard this, she said, "I thought Mrs. Knowles was a lady, but I see she is only a workwoman." A certain sum was paid her, but she was never afterward invited to court. Her avarice increased upon her to such a degree, that she gave up her carriage and horses, her men-servants, and seeing company at her own house ; lived in the meanest manner, and mortified her rich relations in many ways. She loved society, and had numerous invitations to great houses, where her conversation was prized by authors, and artists, and statesmen; but she often arrived with muddy feet, and looking so unlike a guest, that the footman would hardly let her enter. She had a good figure and a sprightly step, even when advanced in years, but her face was very plain. She was returning alone from a grand dinner-party, very late at night, when a well-dressed man, coming up behind her, said he had always wished to kiss a Quakeress and swore he would do it now. She said very calmly, "Wait till we get to that lamp-post, and then if thou wishest to kiss me thou shalt do so." The astonished man obeyed, and when the light fell on her face, he cursed her for an ugly hag and passed on.

Washing cost money in London, and Mrs. Knowles was too miserly to be clean. When invited to meet company at our house, my mother would dress her in her own clothes, and feel herself well rewarded by the conversation of her guest, who was a great politician, and clever men liked to talk with her. She used to say, on meeting my mother, "I know I am too dirty to suit thy company, but I can wear some of thy cast-off clothes, and look very nice."

When on her death-bed, her rich relations, who were around her, were shocked at the state of her chamber, and tried to make it more decent. When she was sleeping heavily, they took off a very dirty counterpane and put on a clean one; but on awaking, she was so distressed by it that they were obliged to let her die under the dirty one.

Her only son inherited not only the accumulated riches of his mother, but also her miserly disposition, and never enjoyed a penny of his fortune.

CHAPTER IV.

ELIZABETH FRY.

MRS. FRY, the reformer of female prisoners in Newgate, was the third daughter of John Gurney, of Earlham Hall, near Norwich, in England. Her family belonged to the Society of Friends, but she alone adhered to their rules and wore their dress. Mr. Gurney had a princely fortune, and made an excellent use of it. He was early left a widower, with eleven children, and never married again. Home education, under his own supervision, was what he chose, and the happy results of his training showed his wisdom. He lived on a large scale, but without ostentation. His mansion was the resort of talent and worth, and all were kindly received from the prince to the beggar. It is told of Mrs. Fry, that when a girl in her teens, a royal prince, son of George III., was her father's guest, and having heard of his dissipated habits, she invited him to leave the gay throng in the drawing-room and accompany her to the school-room, where she made him sit still, while she preached to him in Quaker style. He was too much affected by her discourse to make fun of the interview, and nothing was known of it till long after.

Many suitors were attracted by the elegant simplicity and high culture of the family at Earlham Hall. The stricter Quaker youths paid their court to Elizabeth. Among these were Mr. Joseph Fry, who, like the rest, was rejected, but not utterly discouraged, and hearing that an elderly friend of his was about to pay a visit to Earlham, he told him of this rejected suit and begged him to speak a good word for him. The friend did as desired, and on coming away, he asked Elizabeth what message he should carry to Joseph. She replied, " Tell him, he has no hope, but in the fickleness of woman." " Then I shall tell him he has every hope." And so it proved, he married his lovely Betsy, and transplanted her from the princely establishment and gay family party at Earlham to an old-fashioned house, in a dark court, in the city of London; but this did not disturb the serenity of his wife's well-disciplined mind. She believed that she had been led there by the dictates of that inward monitor whom it was her happiness to listen to and obey, and in her later years she used to ascribe her whole course of usefulness to her fellow-creatures to that union with Joseph Fry and her life in London.

She had been married many years, and was the mother of ten children, when her attention was called to the wretched state of the female prisoners in Newgate by some male friends who went there to see some criminals whom they knew. She was shocked to hear that three hundred women with their numerous children were crowded into four small rooms, without beds or bedding, without classification, tried and untried, in rags and dirt, and there they lived, cooked, and washed. Their wretched condition made them so fierce and brutal, that the governor of the prison entered this portion of it with reluctance, and when Mrs. Fry, accompanied by one other lady, wished to be admitted, he advised them to leave their watches outside, least they should be snatched from them. This they refused to do, and taking with them a quantity of clothing to give away they entered that Babel of discordant sounds.

Their appearance produced a lull, and certainly the tall, commanding figure of Mrs. Fry, with her mild, benignant countenance and her sweet tones of voice, might well make her appear like some heavenly vision to those degraded women. She distributed the clothing, of which they stood so much in need, promised them some comforts, and spoke words of kindness and encouragement to them, such as they rarely, if ever, heard.

Many years after this, I visited Newgate with Mrs. Fry, and witnessed the thorough reformation that had been effected there. The female prisoners were classified, cleanliness and order prevailed, swearing and fighting had given place to reading and sewing, and a committee of ladies were constantly visiting the prison by turns. The morning that I was there, Mrs. Fry was to have her last religious exercises with sixty female convicts, about to embark for Botany Bay. We entered a good sized, clean room, and found them all seated on benches in perfect silence at the farther end of it. Mrs. Fry stood at a small table between her and the convicts, a few visitors like myself, stood on either side of her. She read from the New Testament a few consolatary passages, and then proposed to pray with them. The women rose, turned round, and kneeled beside the benches; Mrs. Fry kneeled on a hassock before her table, and lifted up her melodious voice in such a strain of tender supplication for help and comfort to the afflicted and sorrowful, as I can never forget. She merged herself in them, and seemed as if she were bearing them up on wings of love to the throne of grace. Such a prayer I never before heard, and never shall again. It was sublime, it was divine, and it moved all present to tears. The poor women sobbed aloud.

Mrs. Fry had previously talked with each one of them and given them appropriate advice, and furnished them with employment on their long voyage. My mother used to dress dolls for the convicts' children to play with at sea.

CHAPTER V.

MILFORD HAVEN. — FRENCH SPY. — FRENCH AT FISHGUARD.

THE great success of the sperm-whale fishery in France, and the manufacturing of the best spermaceti candles ever seen in any country, made my father an authority in such matters. Many merchants consulted him, and some statesmen thought it advisable to retain him in England, and induce him to prosecute the fishing there, instead of returning to America. The suit in chancery still lingered along, and he began to listen to the proposals made to him by the Hon. Charles Greville, who had the care of his uncle Sir William Hamilton's estate on the banks of Milford Haven, in South Wales, and earnestly entreated my father to settle there. A visit to the place satisfied him that the port was well adapted to the purpose; but there was no town there, and there were no mechanics capable of fitting out a whaling ship.

Mr. Greville said that if Mr. Rotch would settle there a town would soon be created, and the trades would gather round him, and so it proved.

A large hotel was built, and Mr. Greville's influence caused a custom-house and a post-office to be established there. He granted long leases of land, at very low rents, and houses sprang up like magic. My father had all the land he wanted for warehouses and a dwelling-house, for a mere nominal ground-rent, and Mr. Greville obtained for him all the privileges and bounties that he had enjoyed in France. Several new houses were built before he removed his family to Milford, and one of them, though small, was hired for our use until a larger one could be built.

Coopers, and sailmakers, ship-carpenters, and all the other tradesmen necessary to my father's business, came and settled in Milford, on the prospect of the whale fishery being carried on from that port, and great was the excitement and satisfaction when the first vessel arrived from America loaded with sperm-oil. The cargo was sent round to London in coasting vessels, and the ship was immediately refitted for a voyage to the Pacific Ocean. I have given this account of our settlement in Wales in order to make more intelligible the incidents which linger in my memory and which I am about to relate.

Wales being a conquered country, and the peasantry and yeomanry still speaking a different language from their conquerors, their civilization did not keep pace with that of England. It was allowed to be a hundred years behind, and the manners and customs of all classes were of course very different from those of the English. The Welsh nobility and gentry are very proud of their pedigrees, tracing back their ancestry far beyond the Norman conquest. Many of them have lost much of their ancestral possessions, but none of their pride, and make great efforts to keep up a grand appearance on small means.

It was a great trial to my parents to leave a large circle of congenial friends, and the high state of civilization which London afforded, and plant themselves in a strange land and among such a different kind of people. Mr. Greville gave them letters of introduction to the first families in the country, and wrote to his friends to interest them in us; but still the change was a very painful one.

We were no sooner packed into our small house, in Milford, than Mr. Greville's friends began to call and extend a cordial reception to the new-comers. This was soon followed by notes from several families, saying they would come and dine with us on a certain day. This was an appalling civility to persons not yet settled in their house, and no way prepared to get up a grand dinner. Just arrived, and entirely ignorant of what would be expected of them, they thought it the queerest mode of paying attention to strangers. It must be meant for a civility, and it would not do to refuse it, yet it seemed impossible to accept it. At last my father thought of an excellent way of escaping from the dilemma. He would entertain them at the hotel, he would order the handsomest dinner that could be procured, and the best wines, and not let his guests know his intentions, till they arrived at his house, when a servant should be in attendance to direct them to the hotel.

In this way my mother was relieved of all care and anxiety, and the dinner gave great satisfaction to all parties.

The Welsh nobility live on large estates and in very stately mansions, and their annual visits to London prevent their being so provincial as those who seldom or never visit the metropolis. The descendants of the most ancient families prided themselves on adhering to the old customs of the country, and disdained the idea of importing London fashions and manners. The introduction of railroads has changed all this, and the long journey of two hundred and seventy miles from Milford to London, which used to take ten days to perform, with our own carriage and horses, is now only one day's journey. The roads were ill made and never kept in repair, and this made riding on horseback a favorite mode of conveyance. I have been one of a large dinner-party, to which every guest went on horseback, and all the ladies dined in their cloth habits and rode home many miles at night. Those who possess large landed estates look down upon the inhabitants of country towns, and consider it a condescension to admit to their houses the lawyer, physician, or merchant, though often much better educated than the country squire.

I am thus particular in describing the social state of South Wales because it was the scene of many events which will be better understood in consequence.

I have mentioned a visit which my parents made to South Wales, before settling there, and will now relate some particulars of it which are worthy of notice.

It so happened of all the persons who escaped from France, by hiding themselves in the hold of my father's ship, when he sailed in her from the port of Dunkirk, only one of them ever crossed his path again, and that one was a handsome cabin-boy, transformed into a country squire, married to an heiress, and living on one of her estates. When my father made his tour of observation into Wales, before settling there, he took his wife and his little girl with him and spent several weeks at the Castle Inn, in Haverfordwest. There he did a great deal of writing, and had letters and papers lying about with his name and his address in Dunkirk on them. These circumstances, with his occasionally speaking to his wife and child in French, raised suspicions that he was a French spy, and a paragraph to that effect appeared in a country newspaper, and fell under the eye of the squire. When he read the names of Rotch, and Dunkirk, he began to think that the supposed spy might be the benevolent Quaker who had helped him to escape from France; so he forthwith mounted his dapple-gray steed, and appeared at the Castle Inn. The recognition was, of course, all on one side, for no trace was left of the young cabin-boy, but the meeting was very pleasant and cordial on both sides. He told my father that he was suspected of being a French spy, and that the country was in such fear of French invasion that he might be arrested, if proper precautions were not taken. The squire, being a well-known magistrate, soon put an end to all the false reports about his benefactor, and persuaded him and his wife to become his guests at his country-seat, where he introduced them to his wife and two maiden sisters, all of whom became, in after years, our dear and intimate friends. Many were the happy Christmas days that we spent under that roof, and when, some years after, by my father's advice, and through his interest, the squire became the collector of customs at Milford, the intercourse between his family and ours was constant and agreeable.

The fear of French invasion was not unfounded. Napoleon kept an army at Boulogne, and a flotilla of boats to bring them across the Channel, and he only waited a favorable opportunity to invade England, march to London, and dictate terms of peace from St. James's Palace. This was his plan, but an English fleet kept in the Channel prevented the attempt for many weeks. At length the fleet sailed out of the Channel, and Bonaparte thought that the long-wished for time had arrived. He had previously despatched a few companies of his poorest soldiers to make a landing in South Wales in order to test the loyalty of the Welsh peasantry, whom he falsely supposed to be disaffected towards the English government. They were gone long enough to effect their purpose, when a terrible storm arose which drove the English fleet back into the Channel, and made it impossible for the French army to embark. The unfortunate men sent to make friends with the Welsh landed at a small fishing-town called Fishguard, on a little sandy beach, surrounded by high cliffs. The population was small, and not a soldier in the place, but the inhabitants went to the edge of the cliff to look down. Half of these were women, dressed, according to custom, in men's hats and scarlet cloaks. The French, mistaking them for soldiers, thought their case was hopeless, laid down their arms, and surrendered themselves prisoners of war to the women of Fishguard. A militia regiment, under the command of Lord Cawdor, did arrive in time to take their arms, and march them to Milford, whence they were sent by water to one of the prisons used for French prisoners.

The news of the landing of the French spread like wildfire; people ran for miles, screaming it all the way they went; men on horseback galloped through the land to give the alarm; volunteers, who had been drilled into soldiers, for just such an emergency, thought their time was come for deeds of prowess; armed forces of all descriptions rushed to Fishguard, and there learned that a handful of Frenchmen had surrendered to the old women of Fishguard, and their valor was not needed.

I have heard my mother say that she and her husband were awakened, in the dead of night, by a man calling out, under their window, "Get up, get up, the French have landed, and you will all be murdered in your beds." My father opened the window and asked where they had landed. "At Fishguard," was the reply. "How far off is that?" "Twenty miles." My father returned to bed, saying, "They cannot be here before morning; so we had better get all the sleep we can to-night, for there is no knowing where we may be to-morrow night." They did sleep quietly that night, and the next day heard that the invaders were all made prisoners, and they saw them marched through Milford to be embarked. So ended Napoleon's grand threat of invading England.

CHAPTER VI.

LADY HAMILTON. — LORD NELSON. — CASTLE HALL AND ITS COMPANY.

WHEN Sir William Hamilton returned to England, from his embassy at the court of Naples, he determined to visit his large estate on the banks of Milford Haven, and see the new town which had grown up so suddenly under the good management of his nephew, the Hon. Charles Greville. Lady Hamilton chose to accompany her husband. On hearing this, Lord Nelson became very desirous of examining the celebrated harbor of Milford; so a party was formed for a tour in Wales. Lady Nelson was left behind, and her faithless husband devoted himself to the notorious Lady Hamilton, as if he had been her affianced lover.

Lady Hamilton began her career as a poor girl, selling matches in the streets of London. Happening to pass under the window of Sir Joshua Reynolds, he was so struck with her beauty, that he called her in, and engaged her to sit for her likeness the next day. Having made a charming picture of her, in that character, he found her form so faultless, that he made her his model for other pictures, and at last exhibited her to his fellow artists, and even to amateurs and patrons of art, in chosen attitudes of his arranging, and great was the admiration she excited. One of the spectators fell in love with her beauty, and made her his mistress. Intoxicated by the change from poverty to luxury, she became very extravagant, and the income of her lover would not suffice for her expensive pleasures. He was therefore well pleased when she left him for Sir William Hamilton, then Minister in Naples.

The beautiful match girl now became a very fine lady, and was delighted with the idea of going to Naples and living with a titled ambassador. She had not been long there, when she persuaded her infatuated lover to make her his lawful wife. After this she was presented at that corrupt court, and became the intimate friend of the licentious Queen of Naples. During her residence there, Lord Nelson came, with the English fleet, into that bay so famous for its beauty. The naval hero soon became violently enamored of the charming Lady Hamilton; she too was in love, and for the first time.

Parties and balls on board of Lord Nelson's ship were continually given, to please Lady Hamilton. One day, when she was at a dinner-party there, a naval officer drew his sword, and showing her the spots of blood on it, boasted of how many Frenchmen it had killed. Instead of being disgusted at this brutal conduct, she kissed the sword and passed it round, requesting every one to do the same; but it stopped at a young English traveller, who indignantly refused to touch it.

There was, at this time, a mutiny on board the fleet, and several sailors were hung at the yard-arms of their ships. Lady Hamilton, with a party of her friends, went out in boats to see the executions.

Her amiable old husband had neither eyes nor ears for her intrigues, and always behaved as if he considered her intimacy with Lord Nelson as an affair of pure friendship, in which he participated. He certainly did share in the love-letters, written to Lady Hamilton by Lord Nelson, when he was fighting the French, for he read some of them to my father, and I well remember his repeating the first sentence, in one of them, written the day after a sea-fight. It ran thus: "My dearest, dearest, dearest Emma! last night we sent five hundred Frenchmen's souls to hell." I am not certain of the number specified, but every other word I am sure of. Such was the style of correspondence between the match-girl and the sailor.

When Sir William Hamilton and his party arrived in Milford, accompanied by the great naval commander, the nobility and gentry for miles round flocked to see him, and pay their respects to the hero of the Nile.

A public dinner was given to him, at which Lady Hamilton chose to be present; she sat next to him, cut up his meat, which the loss of an arm prevented him from doing, and fed him with tit-bits from her own plate. She had a fine voice and would sing sailors' songs and verses written in praise of the great admiral, at public dinners, whilst her doting old husband sat by admiring her. When I saw her in 1802, her face was still beautiful, but she had grown fat and her figure was spoiled. Short waists and narrow skirts were then in fashion. The French had introduced the custom of wearing as little clothing as possible, and making that little look like the drapery of an ancient Greek statue. The weather was very warm when Lady Hamilton was in Milford, and she walked about the town in two garments only, showing her shape most indecently.

My mother had resolved to take no notice of Lady Hamilton, and being on the eve of her confinement, she excused herself from calling on her. But that bold woman was resolved that it should not be said that Mrs. Rotch *would not* receive her; so one very warm day, when all our doors and windows stood open, she walked into our drawing-room, where my mother and I were sitting, and greeted us very familiarly. Though I was but a child, I was struck with the coldness of my mother's reception, and wondered that she was not more cordial to such a lovely and fascinating guest.

Lord Nelson was very ordinary in his appearance; lean and sallow, his face much wrinkled and his hair very thin. He was proud of the loss of his arm, and always wore his coat-sleeve empty. When I was one day standing by him, at our house, with my eyes fixed on that empty sleeve, he said, "Look at it well, and then you will always remember me by my one arm." Being in Milford on the first of August, the anniversary of the battle of the Nile, he instituted a boat-race to be held annually, on that day, and Lord Cawdor offered to furnish a silver cup to be run for every year. My father's yacht won it three times, and then he withdrew from the contest, to give others a chance of winning. On these occasions our house was filled with company and we had gay times.

Sir William's estates all descended to his nephews, whether by entail or by his own choice, I do not know; but he left very little to his widow, and Lord Nelson did not add to her income, but made himself ridiculous by a request in his will that the government would grant her a pension. The public could see no reason why the mistress of Lord Nelson should be so provided for, but the friends of the admiral said, she deserved it for having obtained, through her intimacy with the Queen of Naples, some valuable political information for Lord Nelson, when he was commanding a fleet in the Mediterranean. Whether this was true or not, her services were never recognized, and she died, in great poverty, in France.

Lord Nelson gave a full length portrait of himself, in oils, to the hotel at which he stayed in Milford, and which was named for him. The picture hangs there still, though the house has changed hands several times.

Milford enjoyed many years of prosperity under the management of Mr. Greville. Several men-of-war were launched from its dock-yard, daily packets were established between Milford and Waterford, carrying mails and passengers. Militia regiments were quartered there, and the haven was seldom without a vessel of the navy anchored in its roads.

My father was engaged in building a house large enough for his increasing family, when an estate in the neighborhood, of one hundred and eighty acres, with a large house on it, called Castle Hall, was offered for sale, at a very moderate price, and he became the purchaser and removed his family into it. We were all so much pleased with our country life, and my father took so much delight in farming the land, and improving the pleasure-grounds, that the new house in Milford was no inducement to leave it, and we children were rather glad when it was accidentally destroyed by fire.

Seven acres of ornamental grounds and gardens gave my father ample scope for his love of improving and embellishing the place; he made ugly slopes into pretty terraces, formed new land in front of the house, built an orangery eighty feet long and twenty feet high, entirely of iron and glass, and filled it with the finest orange, lemon, and citron-trees from a celebrated orangery in a distant county, sold on the death of the owner. He made pineries too, — three houses, hot, hotter, and hottest, — in which three hundred fine, large pine-apples were produced in one year. The climate was very mild. We had monthly roses blooming out of doors all winter, and a hedge of laurestine, which enclosed a rose-garden, was always in full bloom in February.

All these improvements, with the high cultivation of English gardening, not usually practised in Wales, made Castle Hall a show-place. The orangery and the pinery were a great novelty in Pembrokeshire, and I remember being very tired of showing them to our visitors.

The head-gardener would have complained of

the trouble of showing the place to strangers, had he not been paid by them for doing it. We might well keep the grounds in high order, when a woman could be hired to weed all day for twelve cents, and a laboring man for less than a quarter of a dollar.

My father's hospitality knew no bounds, and our house was filled with the greatest variety of visitors. For months together we never sat down to a meal alone. Besides exchanging visits once or twice a year with the gentry and nobility of the country, we had no objection to the society of the best people in the country towns. After the packets ran from Milford to Waterford, we often had the company of the Irish members of Parliament, on their way to and from London. My father had travelled in Ireland and been treated so hospitably, that he was glad to pay every attention to those who brought letters from his friends in that country.

The long war between France and England prevented the English from travelling on the Continent, and a tour through North and South Wales was an agreeable substitute. Many tourists came, introduced to my father by his London friends; those among them who were artists were especially welcome to my brothers, who enjoyed sketching with them the numerous picturesque castles and ruins to be found in our neighborhood. Every Quaker made our house his home, every American traveller was doubly welcome, and many visited us before the war of 1812. Added to all this variety of guests, there was still another set, entirely distinct from them, who were more to us socially than all the rest. These were very genteel, well-bred people, who, for some reason or other, wished to live retired and very economically for a few years. They occupied three cottages belonging to my father, and bordering on our pleasure-grounds, and were, of course, our nearest neighbors, and became our most intimate friends. My father bought those cottages on purpose to prevent their being inhabited by exceptionable characters, and he was very careful as to whom he let them.

All these various classes of visitors made an immense circle of acquaintances, and we sometimes met with strange experiences among them, one of which will be found in the next chapter.

CHAPTER VII.

HERBERT FAMILY. — SAILOR-BOY. — WANDERING GIRL. — ORLEANS FAMILY.

HOSPITALITY has its dangers, as well as its pleasures, and so my parents found, when a guest, invited only to dine, was confined to their house for three months by acute rheumatism, and a determination to continue in good quarters. We were then living at Castle Hall.

Returning home from London in the mail-coach, my father met with an Irish artist, named Herbert, whose conversation amused him much, and finding that he took small full-length likenesses, in water colors, he invited him to his house to make a picture of my mother.

Herbert came and spent a month in making frightful likenesses of the whole family, and was a very acceptable guest to the younger members of it, for he aided us in getting up private theatricals, and gave us many pleasant evenings, reading aloud to us the best English comedies. A year after this, he was on his way to Ireland with his wife and daughter, and they were all invited to dine at our house. On rising from the table,

Mrs. Herbert was seized with violent pains in her limbs, and could hardly move. My mother kindly advised her being put to bed and having hot fomentations, little thinking that her suffering guests would be the torment of the house for three months to come, but so it fell out.

Mr. Herbert had married his wife for her handsome figure, without any knowledge of her character, and found himself united to a vixen, who tyrannized over him and his children in the most remorseless way. He was very good-tempered, devoted to his art, and yielded to her rule for the sake of peace. Her violent temper, exasperated by the pain of acute rheumatism, made her so exacting and unreasonable that the devoted attendance of her husband and daughter, and of our excellent servants, could not soothe or satisfy her. Our family physician attended her, and prescribed a low diet, but this she secretly evaded. Bountiful dinners used to be sent up to her daughter Lucy, a girl of fourteen, whom she would not allow to leave her room, and of these the mother ate by far the larger part; when she was satisfied, the plate was put before her pug-dog, and what he left, was all that Lucy had. This had gone on for a long while, and the poor child was half starved before my mother discovered it; when she did, she required Lucy's presence at the dinner-table, and there she always came until, one day, she sent word she could not come. My sister, about the same age as Lucy, was sent up to know the reason why, and came down in tears, to say that the poor girl's ears had been pulled so violently by her mother, that they were bleeding, and she could not come down. The presence of Mr. Herbert alone prevented the explosion of our wrath and indignation, but we were all much excited against this unnatural mother. My father told Mr. Herbert that he ought not to allow his daughter to be so ill-treated ; the poor man said he could not help it, that Lucy was ill-tempered and obstinate, and her mother had never loved her, because she was so ugly. This was to us a new view of maternal feelings.

Soon after all supplies of hearty food were cut off Mrs. Herbert's severe pains left her, and the fever subsided ; but she still kept her bed, and slept so much by day, that she often lay awake at night, and then she would not let Lucy sleep, but kept her standing by her bedside, and when her sleepy eyes closed, she would pinch her to keep her awake. We had observed black and blue spots on Lucy's arms, but it was not till she ventured to confide her griefs to my sister, that we knew how she came by them. One day on seeing my sister kiss her mother, Lucy burst into tears, and said she never had kissed her mother, and should no more think of it, than of kissing the Queen. Treated with kindness, for the first time in her life, Lucy became a new being. Talents were developed that astonished her father. Seeing me draw heads in crayon, she borrowed my materials and made a very tolerable likeness of me. Seeing my sister write verses, she tried to do the same, and succeeded so well that her father could not believe the verses to be hers; he was sure she had copied them from some book; but when she wrote some lines, impromptu, on an event that had just happened, he was obliged to give up the idea inculcated by his wife, that Lucy was the worst and most stupid of children. He now thought it worth while to give her lessons in drawing, with a view to her future maintenance; but her mother interrupted them, and would not let Lucy perform the work which her father required of her. As soon as he left the house she would make Lucy leave her drawing and sit in her room, and then tell her father that Lucy left it voluntarily. The poor child dare not gainsay her mother, but one of her young friends told Mr. Herbert the truth about it, and he ceased scolding her.

Mrs. Herbert had been well enough for a month to pass most of her time down stairs, to take drives, and to walk about the grounds, before any sign of departure was made. My mother bore the trial without a complaint, but the patience of the servants was nearly exhausted before the three Herberts, with their lap-dog and canary-bird, departed for Ireland. One Saturday afternoon, in January, they embarked on board the sailing-packet, which ran between Milford and Waterford, well provisioned by my mother for their short voyage. Mr. Herbert expressed his sincere gratitude, and Lucy was heart-broken at leaving her only friends, but Mrs. Herbert seemed only provoked at having to go away at all. Our carriage took them to Milford, and my father saw them on board the packet, and privately urged upon Mr. Herbert the necessity of separating Lucy from her mother.

Did not we talk them over that evening, and lament over the fate of that unhappy girl! As the next day was Sunday, the housemaid was excused from doing anything to the two rooms which they had occupied, and which were in such a plight as to require whitewashers and painters to make them decent. A very unusual sight for that part of South Wales awaited us the next morning; the ground was covered with snow, and the storm continuing, no one went to church. We were all in the library reading or writing, and enjoying such tranquillity as we had not had for three months, when on looking out of the window my brother exclaimed, "Here they all are coming back." We thought he was joking, but it was too true; there was father, mother, daughter, dog, and canary-bird, all ploughing through the snow up to our door! We swallowed down our chagrin, and tried to receive them hospitably. We were assisted in this by the real regret expressed by Mr. Herbert, and by the sufferings of Lucy, whose hands were nearly frozen by carrying the bird-cage. They told us that the storm had driven back the packet, and the tide was so low they could not land at Milford, nor indeed anywhere but on a long point of land belonging to our estate. This remarkable necessity helped to reconcile us to their return, and the housemaid was glad enough that nothing had been done to their rooms.

They stayed with us only a few days and then took lodgings at Milford, as Mrs. Herbert was afraid to try another voyage at that inclement season. All my mother's servants and children had been strictly charged not to speak of Mrs. Herbert's faults to any one out of the house; so the inhabitants of Milford were well disposed towards them, but they had not been there long before an old friend of ours said to my mother, "What crime have you ever committed, that you should have such an infliction as three months of Mrs. Herbert's company? Why, she is a perfect Xantippe! How could you bear with her for three months? The woman in whose house they are has given them warning to quit, on account of Mrs. Herbert's treatment of her daughter. She struck her with a carving-knife and cut a gash in her cheek. All the town is in a ferment about it."

When the spring came the Herberts went to Ireland, and Lucy was placed in a convent, but that dreadful life of inaction and monotony was worse for her mind than her mother's ill treatment; she became insane and was removed to an asylum in Dublin, where she died in a few years. She wrote to my sister, from the convent, very interesting letters, though containing illusions which showed her mind to be unsound. She begged my sister to procure for her a passage to America, in one of her father's ships, as she had received a Divine command to go to that country and preach the importance and efficacy of love. All sectarian differences were to be done away in that new land of freedom, and the gospel of love was to be the only doctrine preached. A beautiful idea this for an ill-educated Roman Catholic girl to originate. She never could have heard it where she was.

I remember, when living in Milford, seeing my mother in the kitchen talking with a very pretty young sailor, who said he belonged to a vessel in the harbor, bound to New York, and hearing that an American family resided in this house, he called to offer to carry out letters for them. An extraordinary piece of courtesy thought my mother. She asked him what brought him on shore. — "To get water for the ship from a neighboring spring; the boat's crew are filling casks there now." Observing his delicate white hands, and struck with his good language and gentle voice, she suspected him to be a runaway school-boy, and taxed him with it. He blushingly denied it. She said those hands do not look as though they had ever handled tarry ropes. He pulled down the sleeves of his jacket to hide them and looked embarrassed. She asked him if his mother knew where he was, and he hesitatingly said she did not. On this my mother depicted the anguish of a parent under such circumstances, and exhorted him to write to her before he slept, and tell her where he was going, which he promised to do. By way of seeing him again my mother said she would write by him to her friends in America, and he promised to call for her letter. Several days passed and he did not appear; but we heard a strange report from the neighboring town that a young lady, in sailor's clothes, had been found on board an American vessel in the harbor, and that a gentleman had arrived, travelling post, with four horses, had gone on board the vessel and brought off a lady whom he carried away with him. The mystery of my mother's sailor-boy was solved, and she soon received a letter from the runaway girl, thanking her for the good advice she had given her, and saying, that the letter she wrote to her mother, expecting to sail before it was received, had been the means of saving her from a ridiculous adventure, of which she was now heartily ashamed. She proved to be of a highly respectable family in Bristol, whom my mother knew. There was no love in the case, it was merely the freak of a young person who was tired of a very monotonous life.

I know a somewhat similar case in the family of my friend R—— B——. The youngest of seven daughters fancied herself less loved and less cared for than her sisters, and, in a fit of discontent, walked off one fine morning from her luxurious home, and without purse or scrip, or any definite plan, wandered on till dark, enjoying the idea of the sensation her disappearance would create at home. She applied for a lodging at the house of a small farmer, but was told they did not take in trampers. This surprised her, for she had read of heroines in distress who always received kindness from strangers. It was a warm night, and she laid down on some straw she found in a shed and slept till morning. She arose very hungry but walked on till she came to another small house, where, after asking her many questions, she was given a very good breakfast. When she rose to go, she found herself a prisoner; the family had discovered who she was, and she was detained, not very unwillingly, until a brother and sister arrived in their close carriage to take her home. Her desire to create a sensation in the dull life of the great house, was fully gratified by the accounts she heard of the alarm of her family, and the active search made for her all night. She fared the better for this *escapade*, and more care was taken to promote her happiness.

When girls have finished their school education, and have no inclination to pursue their studies, they should be provided with some necessary and constant employment to save them from the *ennui* which led to both the absurd enterprises above related.

During the exile of the Orleans family, two brothers of Louis Philippe made the tour of Wales, and brought letters of introduction to my father, then living in Milford. He gave them a dinner, and as my parents had been in France during the troubles that drove them into exile, they had much interesting conversation together. I was then ten years old, and had been reading in French *Le Théâtre d'Education* of Madame de Genlis, and was greatly excited by seeing the children whom she educated, the very Theodore whom I had read of. I kept whispering to my mother, "Ask about Madame de Genlis." At last she did inquire after her, and I well remember the answer of the Duc de Montpensier. "I owe much to that artful woman." I was disappointed and shocked, for I thought if he owed her much he need not speak ill of her.

The Duc de Montpensier was in a consumption, and died not long after his tour in Wales.

Madame de Genlis lived to old age, and passed her last years as a boarder in a convent several miles from Paris. She used to boast that she could do twenty things, by any one of which she could earn a living, and to say that in an age of continual revolutions every one should be so prepared.

CHAPTER VIII.

CRABBE. — BUXTON. — JOANNA BAILLIE.

A CURIOUS circumstance in the life of Crabbe the poet, not mentioned in his biography, is connected with the inhabitants of one of my father's cottages. A widow lady and her two daughters lived there several years, and were very intimate with our family. One of the ladies was engaged to the poet, and was jilted by him when on the point of being married and having the wedding-breakfast at our house.

The beginning of the affair is as remarkable as its termination; so I will relate the whole. Miss Charlotte P., the accomplished daughter of a wealthy owner of mines in Cornwall, interested herself in those unhappy creatures whose lives are spent underground, and finding among them a romantic case of love and constancy, she sent the story to Mr. Crabbe, the popular poet of the day, considering it especially suited to his style of composition. He was pleased with the narrative and charmed by the letter which accompanied it. A very agreeable correspondence followed, which lasted several months. Miss P. was engaged to be married, and her affianced was often at the house, and always read Crabbe's letters to her. He thought them nothing less than love-letters, and advised her to drop the correspondence. She laughed at the idea, and believed he had a wife living; her lover thought he was a widower, and insisted upon it that he was making love to Miss P. She would not agree to that, but was very ready to drop the correspondence. The very next letter from the aged poet was a declaration of love, and a proposal to visit her! Great was the rallying and joking which Miss P. had to endure. She was provoked with herself and the poet, and wished she had never sent him the story of the miner. She begged a friend who was staying with her, Miss Charlotte R., to write to Mr. Crabbe, and inform him of her engagement. The friend did so in the most kind and flattering way, and received a very remarkable answer.

Mr. Crabbe was so much pleased with the friend's letter, that he transferred his proposals from the first Charlotte to the second; he was sure they were kindred spirits, and as he had not seen either lady, it would make no difference to him! This was too good a joke to be kept secret, and a large family party were greatly diverted by it. After all sorts of fun had been made of it, Charlotte the second was observed to look very grave, and not to join in the diversion of the party. She gave them a second fit of astonishment by accepting the poet's offer, and appointing a meeting with him at the house of her aunt, in a neighboring county. They met, were mutually pleased, and parted betrothed to each other.

On her return home we were soon informed of her engagement to Mr. Crabbe, but were charged not to mention it before her mother. "Why not," was of course asked, and her reply was, "Because my mother is so old-fashioned that she would call my dear bard my *sweetheart*, and talk about *courtship*, and you know I could not bear that; it would be insupportable."

With all this nonsense she was sincerely attached to Mr. Crabbe, and kept up a brisk correspondence with him. At first she would read parts of his letters to me, and talk incessantly of him and his poems. She was very proud of her engagement to so celebrated a poet. After some months had elapsed, a time was fixed for the marriage, and then it was deferred by Mr. Crabbe for some slight reason. My father wrote to the "dear bard," and invited him to stay at his house when he should come to be married to Miss C. R., but received no reply. Charlotte looked unhappy, but still her preparations went on. I was asked to make up the wedding favors, which were bows of white satin ribbon, edged round with narrow silver fringe; the white gloves were bought which were to be given to the wedding-guests; our cook had made the wedding-cake; when we were startled by the news that the match was broken off, and Charlotte was in fits.

It appeared afterwards that Crabbe's grown up sons convinced him of the folly of his conduct; he had long repented of his sudden engagement, and had tried by his correspondence so to displease the lady, as to make her break it off. She was resolved to have the *éclat* of marrying a celebrated poet, and would take no hints to the contrary. She was also in love with her old bard, and never recovered from her chagrin and sorrow. She died in a few years, and her family always believed that her life was shortened by this affair.

My most intimate friend from childhood to old age was a Miss H., who resided near London, and in her middle age she formed a great friendship for Mr. Crabbe. He was rector of a parish at Trowbridge, a few miles from the city of Bath, where Miss H. spent part of every winter and had much of her friend's company. Happening to be in Bath, I was invited to a ceremonious breakfast given by Miss H., and was much pleased with the idea of meeting several literary characters, and among them Mr. Crabbe; but before the day came, I was earnestly requested to stay away from that breakfast. Mr. Crabbe could not meet a person so intimately connected with the lady he had jilted. This was soon after that unpleasant affair. Many years afterwards we became very good friends, and it happened thus: —

I was staying at the house of Miss H., near London, when Crabbe was expected to make his annual visit. I offered to go away, but my friend would not hear of it; she was determined that her two most intimate friends should know and like each other. He was in London, and Miss H. was to bring him out in her carriage, and she made me go into town with her. When we stopped at his lodgings, the old gentleman clambered into the carriage as though every joint was stiffened by age. When at last he plumped down on the seat and looked around him, my friend introduced me. He started as if electrified. I said, "I am very happy to see Mr. Crabbe"; he replied very crossly, "Yes, we always like to see those we have heard a great deal about." — "It is Mr. Crabbe the poet that I am glad to see." — "O! I thank you for that," and he seized my hand and shook it heartily. In a few days we had talked over the whole affair of Miss Charlotte, and he ended by saying, "I know I behaved very badly, but I should have done worse if I had married her."

At the same house where I met Mr. Crabbe I

used frequently to see that honest statesman, Fowell Buxton. A grand *physique* corresponded to his noble mind, and his powerful frame set off to advantage the gentleness of his domestic character. I saw him the very day that he risked his life by seizing and holding a mad dog that was carrying danger and dismay into a populous street. I remember my friend's examining his hands to see if there were any scratch on them by which the poison might have entered.

My parents were acquainted with the grandmother of Mr. Buxton, and used to hear her give very entertaining accounts of visits she received from George III. and his family when they were in the habit of going every summer to Weymouth for sea-bathing. Mrs. Buxton had a fine country-house without the town, and lived there in ease and affluence. The king took a fancy to honor her and amuse himself by dining, not with her, but at her house, once during his stay at Weymouth. The queen and princesses chose to accompany him, so, although the king ate nothing but beefsteak, a luxurious dinner must be prepared for the royal ladies. Mrs. Buxton never knew when they were coming till the morning of the day chosen by his Majesty, and as he required a very early dinner it was no easy matter to be prepared for him and his family. The grandchildren of Mrs. Buxton said they fared sumptuously every day during the King's stay in Weymouth, until his visit was over, for they ate up the good things kept in readiness for the royal party.

On one of his visits the King came a little before the dinner-hour, and took a fancy to go over Mrs. Buxton's nice house. She hoped that he meant only the lower floor, for all her chambers were in dire confusion, every member of the family having dressed in great haste for the occasion. No one could precede the King, and, to her dismay, up stairs he went. There was a housemaids' closet in sight, and into it had run two housemaids, to avoid being seen. The King perceived that the door moved a little, and he attempted to open it; the women held on to it, resolved not to be seen; but when it occurred to them that they were resisting their King, they suddenly let go, and his Majesty narrowly escaped falling backward. He laughed, and went on, looking into every room and praising the house.

In those days, Royalty was never waited on by hired menials, nor could a subject sit at the same table with the King's family; so the hostess stood beside the Queen all through the dinner, and her grandchildren waited on her guests. They had funny times rehearsing as footmen, and learning how to change plates and hand the liquors. It would seem to us a very doubtful honor thus to entertain crowned heads.

Another celebrated person whom I used to meet at the house of Miss H., and with whom I have often dined at her own modest mansion in Hampstead, was Joanna Baillie. She was past fifty when I first saw her, and appeared an old lady to me, then in my teens. She dressed like an aged person, and with scrupulous neatness. She lived with a sister who looked older still, because she had not the vivacity of Joanna, and was only distinguished for the amiability with which she bore being outshone by her more gifted relative.

Miss Baillie, according to the English custom, took the title of Mrs. Joanna Baillie, on passing her fiftieth birthday. She gave the prettiest and the pleasantest dinners, and presided at them with peculiar grace and tact, always attentive to the wants of her guests, and yet keeping up a lively conversation the while. She took such pleasure in writing poetry, and especially in her plays on the Passions, that she said, "If no one ever read them, I should find my happiness in writing them."

Though she was young when she left her native land, she never lost her Scotch accent. I thought it made her conversation only the more piquant. She was full of anecdote and curious facts about remarkable people. I only recollect her telling one of Lord Byron being obliged, by politeness, to escort her and her sister to the opera, and her perceiving that he was provoked beyond measure at being there with them, and that he made faces as he sat behind them.

CHAPTER IX.

LADY MACWORTH.

AN acquaintance of twenty years with the subject of the following story makes me certain of all the facts as here given.

There lived in the town of Swansea, in South Wales, a widow lady, with one daughter, who was a great beauty, very high-spirited, and somewhat spoiled by indulgence. At seventeen she was the toast of the whole county, to use the phrase of the day, and surrounded by admirers and lovers. A certain Baronet, possessed of a charming country-seat in the vicinity of the town, fell violently in love with Miss M——. She refused him; but he would not take no for an answer, and persecuted her with attentions. She loved no one else, and her mother favored his suit. Young as she was, and under the influence of an ambitious mother, she yet had an idea that she ought to *love* the man she married, and for a long time she persisted in rejecting Sir Herbert Macworth's suit. He became desperate, and presented himself before her with a loaded pistol, swearing he would shoot himself in her presence if she gave him no hope; she was so alarmed that she hardly knew what she said, but she prevented him from committing suicide that day. After many more scenes of violence, she was worried into compliance, and became the wife of a very dissipated and half-crazy man. He drove tandem in an open carriage, every pannel and each wheel painted a different color, and on the back were the words, *This is the Tippee.*

Installed as Lady Macworth and mistress of the Knoll, which was the name of his country-seat, her only company were Sir Herbert's riotous companions, who, according to the custom of that day, spent the evening in drinking and carousing, and, when the guests were carried home by their servants, the host was generally prostrate on the floor, to be picked up and put to bed by his valet and footmen. The young wife was shocked by these excesses, but could not make Sir Herbert ashamed of them; for a night's sleep obliterated from his mind the scene of the previous evening. It occurred to her that he had better be made acquainted with the state in which he and the room were, when the carouse broke up; so the next time that her husband was dead-drunk on the floor, she forbade the servants to remove him or anything about him. Broken glass and spilled wine and chairs upset were all left as they were, and she locked up the dining-room door, resolved that Sir Herbert should remain there till morning. Finding the men-servants were inclined to disobey her, she mounted guard over the room with a pistol in her hand, and declared she would shoot the man who dared approach that door. On this the servants went off to bed, and she kept her melancholy watch alone.

As soon as it was broad daylight she entered the room, opened the shutters, and aroused her husband. His astonishment and bewilderment were great, and when he came to his senses he was shocked at the scene around him, and began to blame his servants. She told him the part she had acted and her motive for so doing; and he was so pleased with her courage and spirit, that he called her a fine girl and promised never to repeat such an orgy.

She made him give up some of his worst companions, and invited to her house the best of her friends; but she could not reform such a poor, weak, half-crazy man, and he did not live long to torment her. She became a widow at nineteen, and sent for a dear friend, a few years older than herself, to come and live with her. Miss P—— was a woman of good sense and high principles. She had renounced her young friend when she made a match so unworthy of her; but now that that terrible alliance was dissolved, she hoped to be of some service to her, and became a resident at the Knoll. Her influence was very powerful, and the lovely young widow corrected many of her faults, ceased to use the slang and coarse expressions which her husband had taught her, closed her doors to his bad companions, cultivated the society of the best people, and became the amiable and elegant woman that she was when I first knew her.

During her husband's life there came to her house a young man of high family, large fortune, and great beauty. He was making the tour of Wales, and brought a letter of introduction to Sir Herbert Macworth. He was heir to large estates, and his mother was urging him to marry. He said he must first fall in love, and he had never yet seen the lady whom he could love. When he left her, to make this tour, she hoped he would be captivated by some fair Cambrian, and return to her engaged. On his coming home, she eagerly asked him if he had seen the lady he could love; he answered very gravely that he had, but she was already the wife of another, and therefore he should never marry. He had fallen in love with Lady Macworth! To divert the current of his thoughts he went abroad, and only returned when he heard of the death of Sir Herbert Macworth. In due time he renewed his acquaintance with the lovely widow, and was delighted to find her so improved; attractive as she had been before, she was now tenfold more charming. She was cultivating her mind by reading the best books, and improving her character by listening to the counsel of her excellent friend, Miss P——. He joined in their pursuits, and enlarged the boundaries of their knowledge by his instructive conversation. The hearts of the two young people were soon united, but she refused to engage herself to him until she had been a widow for a year. This deference she paid to the opinion of the world. At the expiration of the year he urged her to marry him; but she said she would not marry until she was twenty-one years old. "I have never yet been my own mistress; as a minor I have no power over my property, and I choose to be of age before I again give myself a master."

In vain did her lover combat this fancy, and assure her she should do as she pleased with her property after marriage. She put him off for another year, and enjoyed meanwhile as much as she could of his society. A life-long grief was the consequence of this delay, for her lover died toward the close of that year; and she always believed that, had she married him, he would not have been exposed to the infectious disease which killed him.

Now, for the first time, did she experience the true heart-sorrow of a widow. She renounced society, shut herself up with her friend, and suffered severely from this bereavement. The near relations of Mr. Hanbury had paid her great attention as his affianced bride, and she was much beloved by his mother and brother. For many months they were the only friends admitted to her privacy. Their sympathy consoled and cheered her. This younger brother succeeded to the estates of the one that was gone; he resembled him in his person and character; their voices were alike, and their pursuits the same. Can we think it very strange if this living likeness should, in time, take the place of the original, if words of love should mingle with words of sympathy, and the same tones that once vibrated through her heart should again find an answering chord there?

In marrying the younger Mr. Hanbury, she took possession of the same delightful home that she would have shared with his elder brother, the same woods and groves and brooks that were sacred to his memory, and her love for his name induced her to relinquish her title of Lady Macworth and become plain Mrs. Hanbury. One of her first occupations after her marriage was to build a pretty hermitage on a high point of land in her park, which commanded a view of the church where the remains of her first love were laid. She, with the aid of Miss P——, covered the inside walls with shells and spars and other brilliant stones. The floor was of very small pebbles, blue and white, laid in a regular pattern and producing a very pretty effect.

When I was shown the curious and elaborate work bestowed on this little building by the delicate hands of Mrs. Hanbury, I called it a labor of patience. "Say rather a labor of love; it did me more good to work here than anything else could do, and I was only sorry when it was finished." She loved her husband, but it was with a chastened, sober love, which showed how much she had suffered.

CHAPTER X.

PRINCESS CARABOO.

I WAS on a visit near Bristol when the following events took place, and I shared in the excitement they produced.

Mrs. Worrell, a lady of fortune, residing at her country-seat, just out of Bristol, in England, saw, coming up her avenue, a fine-looking young woman, strangely dressed, and beckoned to her to come to the drawing-room window, instead of going round to the back-door. The stranger bowed gracefully, but did not speak. Mrs. Worrell made some kind inquiries, but was answered in some language unknown to her. She soon found, however, that the poor girl was hungry, and sent her round to her kitchen to be refreshed with good food. While eating it, a sailor came begging to the door, saying he had been shipwrecked, and lost everything, on his return voyage from India. It occurred to Mrs. Worrell that he might understand the language of the poor girl, and, on bringing them together, he said she spoke the Malay language, and he understood it a little, and interpreted her story thus: "She was a native of one of the Malay Islands, but somehow or other had become a servant in an English family in Calcutta, and accompanied them on their return to England. The captain of the vessel fell in love with her, and when they got into port, she was so afraid of his carrying her off, that she stripped off her clothes and swam ashore. At the first house she went to, the people clothed her as you see. The Malay women swim and dive as well as the men."

This history, with the interesting appearance of the girl, so touched the benevolent heart of Mrs. Worrell, that she resolved to give her a home for the present, and sent off the sailor well paid for serving as her interpreter. The sons of Mrs. Worrell were not so easily satisfied as to the story of this new inmate, and even suggested that she might be an impostor, or the agent of a gang of thieves, all which suppositions their mother indignantly rejected. There was in the house a volume of costumes of the Malays, and on showing them to the stranger, her face brightened up, and she made signs that these were her people; and when she came to the costume of a Malay princess, she was much excited, and indicated that it was herself. The dress was formed of a quantity of fine white muslin, with a rich sash of various colors round the waist, drapery hanging from the shoulders nearly to the feet, a curious head-dress of red muslin, with a bunch of peacock's feathers sticking up on one side. A pair of sandals completed the costume. Mrs. Worrell furnished all the materials for her strange guest to dress herself in this manner, and in a few days she was introduced to Mrs. Worrell's friends as the Princess Caraboo, and was allowed to associate with the family as an equal. Her dark complexion and shining black hair, large lustrous eyes and black eyebrows, gave her a very Oriental appearance, and her costume was very becoming. It was soon known that there was a Malay princess staying at Mrs. Worrell's, and her door was besieged with visitors, curious to see this novelty, and all went away satisfied that she was really the Princess Caraboo. She bore being stared at, and talked about, with such dignity and propriety as astonished all who saw her. Mrs. Worrell observed that her not understanding English helped her to bear it. Many were so charmed with her as to think her a great beauty, and all extolled her grace and delicacy.

In her morning walks with her hostess, she would surprise her by running up a tree like a cat, or diving into a pond, or turning a somerset on the road, — strange pranks for a drawing-room guest, but supposed to be in character for a Malay princess. Caraboo was requested to write her language, which she did, and the manuscript was sent to Oxford, to ascertain what language it was, and found to be unknown. All those circumstances were told in the papers, and people came in crowds to see this wonderful foreigner, and poor Mrs. Worrell was getting tired of her *lion*, when, on going to breakfast one morning, Caraboo was not to be found. The poor girl had perceived that her kind hostess was worried, and determined to relieve her of her presence; so she stripped herself of all the fine clothes and trinkets that had been given to her, and, putting on the old clothes in which she first entered the house, she ran away at early dawn, and for several days eluded the pursuit of her kind friend, who could not bear the idea of her becoming again a destitute beggar.

She was at last found, and brought back to her luxurious home, and made more of than ever, her conduct having proved her honesty and delicacy. Various were the opinions entertained of this wonderful stranger; sarcastic paragraphs in the newspapers ridiculed all her admirers as the dupes of an impostor; spirited defences of her were written, and it was observed that it was only those who had never *seen* her that doubted the reality of her character. All who came within reach of her personal attractions were firm believers in the Princess Caraboo.

Worn out by living in this state of continual

exhibition, her health failed, and she was confined to her bed in a high fever. Several physicians attended her, and came believing her an impostor, and that she understood English as well as they did; so they determined to put her to the proof, by narrowly watching her countenance when they spoke to each other of her dangerous illness, and that nothing could save her life. They said all this, and much more, without producing the least change in her countenance, and then they became believers in the Malay Princess. The fever did not give way to their treatment, and fears were really entertained for her life. But she took the case into her own hands, and eluding the vigilance of her nurse, she ran up into the garret and plunged into a large tank of cold water. After the whole family had searched for her, there she was found, cured of her fever, for from that time she recovered.

So many persons were disappointed of seeing her, during her illness, that fewer now came to the house; but still the controversy concerning her continued in the newspapers; and one middle-aged man of the world, who prided himself on his knowledge of the female mind, said he knew he could detect her as an impostor, if he could be alone with her for half an hour.

The challenge was accepted by Mrs. Worrell. He came to Bristol, he had his *tête-à-tête* with

Caraboo, he tried all his arts, and failed to prove her to be anything but a Malay girl who did not understand English. He said he had flattered her and made love to her; he had acted the fatherly friend, and assured her that he knew her true history, and that she understood every word he said; and all this did not change the expression of her face from that of stupid wonderment at his behavior. He ended by saying, "I am sure she thinks me either a mountebank or a fool, I don't know which."

Caraboo had many invitations to visit the neighboring gentry, but she declined them all, and only accepted one from a celebrated physician in Bath, who shared Mrs. Worrell's faith in her as a Princess, and wished to show her to his friends. The poor girl was so worn out when she arrived at his house that she retired early; and a party of young ladies who called to see her were so disappointed to hear that she was in bed, that they begged leave to see her asleep. Having waited till she was supposed to sleep soundly, they ventured into her room. One hand hung carelessly over the edge of the bed, and her visitors were so interested in her, that each one kneeled down and kissed it. Her visit to Bath was short, for she was weary of being exhibited.

Soon after her return to Bristol, she was sitting with Mrs. Worrell by the drawing-room window, which commanded a view of the avenue, and saw a woman coming up who filled her with alarm. She screamed, threw herself on her knees before Mrs. Worrell, and exclaimed, in good English, "O, Mrs. Worrell, hear me first." To hear her speak so upset Mrs. Worrell; she nearly fainted, and could hear no more. The structure which she had been weeks in rearing was suddenly demolished, and she felt as if the solid earth were giving way under her.

Caraboo's real story was this. She was born a Gypsy, and after leading their vagrant life till she was seventeen, she struck out a new path for herself, and became a house-servant. She was clever, active, and faithful, and went out with a family to the East Indies, and, after various vicissitudes, found herself reduced to beggary in the streets of Bristol. This was just after the fall of Napoleon, and the peace between France and England, which brought over many French beggars, and she observed that they received more alms than she did. So she tried to make herself look foreign, and pretended not to speak English. On first trying this she wandered as far as Mrs. Worrell's, and we have seen what happened there. It remains to be explained that the sailor knew nothing of the Malay language; but having said he did, and supposing that her gibberish was that language, he felt obliged to pretend to interpret it, and she, hearing the story that he made up for her, adopted it, never imagining all that it entailed upon her. When she ran away it was because she was tired of acting a part, but was forced back into it. When she heard the physicians say she would die, it did not disturb her, for she was tired of life. When the man of fashion had his interview with her, she was fully prepared for him by having heard it talked of before her, but she certainly had a wonderful command of countenance. She said nothing had ever tried her so much as those ladies in Bath kissing her hand; she came very near bursting out laughing.

All whom she had deceived were grievously mortified, and some were enraged; but Mrs. Worrell, who had a right to feel worse than anybody, behaved in the kindest manner to her poor *protégée*. She was conscious of having done much to force upon her the part she had acted, and she kindly shielded her from all unpleasant consequences. The Malay costume was changed for a decent English dress, and a plan was laid to send her out to a Moravian settlement in the United States. The manager of the Bristol theatre wished to engage her as an actress, and intended to have her story made into a farce, and that she should act Caraboo on his stage. To this Mrs. Worrell would not listen for a moment, and the gratitude of the Gypsy girl making her conform to the wishes of her kind friend, she went to America. I have still to explain why the sight of that woman in the avenue so affected Caraboo. She recognized her as the person in whose house she had passed a night, and to whom she owed the price of her lodging. A particular description of the beggar-girl, as she first appeared to Mrs. Worrell, had been put in the newspaper, and the lodging-house keeper recognized in it her runaway lodger, and traced her to her luxurious home.

Since writing the above, I have seen the following paragraph: —

"English papers mention the death at Bristol of an importer of leeches, who, when a young and prepossessing girl, had for a short time created a great sensation in the literary and fashionable circles of Bath and other places, under the false title and rank of 'the Princess Caraboo.'"

CHAPTER XI.

THE ENGLISH STAGE. — MRS. JORDAN.

WHEN I was young, I used to hear a very old gentleman boast of having seen Garrick perform, and express some contempt for all other actors. Now that I am old, I congratulate myself on having seen all three of the Kembles, Mrs. Siddons and her two brothers, act all their best parts, previous to Mrs. Siddons retiring from the stage. I also saw the *début* of Miss O'Neil on the London boards, and witnessed the triumph of her natural acting over the artificial, conventional manner of the Kemble school. At first, a London audience did not know what to make of an actress whose style was entirely different from that of Mrs. Siddons; but when her pathos drew tears from all eyes, and her emotion stirred every heart, old prejudices gave way, and the applause was rapturous. I saw her in the play of "The Stranger," three nights in succession, and could see the growing enthusiasm of the audience for her new style of acting. Her career on the stage was short, for she married well and retired to private life.

Her marriage happened in this way. There was at Kilkenny, in Ireland, a company of amateur actors, who performed for a week every year, for the benefit of the poor; and as it was deemed highly improper, in those days, for ladies to take parts with them, they hired professional actresses. Miss O'Neil was invited to act there; she consented, and gave her services to her countrymen. Two brothers of a noble family were among the best performers, and they acted the principal male characters to Miss O'Neil's female ones. These plays were very fashionable, and people came from far and near to attend them. When they were over, one of those brothers sought an interview with the other, and said he was about to tell him something which he knew he would object to very strongly, — that he meant to marry Miss O'Neil; she had accepted his offer, and nothing should prevent his making her his wife. The brother replied, "I have but one objection to your doing so, and that is, that I meant to marry her myself." The friends of these young men were at first opposed to the match; but the excellent qualities of Miss O'Neil, and her judicious conduct, overcame their dislike, and she became an honored and loved member of the family.

Very different was the career of the unhappy Mrs. Jordan. Comedy was her forte, and she was as natural in it as Miss O'Neil was in tragedy.

She drew crowded houses, and fascinated the public by her gayety and humor, her sprightliness and grace, her pretty face and delicate form. The Duke of Clarence, one of the handsome sons of George III., fell in love with her, when she was at the height of her fame and in the bloom of youth. After a long series of flattering attentions, he succeeded in carrying her off to his fine country-house in the environs of London, and made her the mistress of himself and his establishment. For several years she continued her professional career, and paid her lover's debts with the emolument. Her influence made him a domestic character, and a large family of children attached him to his home, and made the union seem like that of a married pair. After having several children she left the stage and devoted herself to the government of her family and the education of her daughters, who were most carefully brought up. One of her regulations was that they should never look into a newspaper.

I happened to be visiting at a country-seat, near that of the Duke of Clarence, and where the young ladies of the family were taking French lessons from the same master who was teaching the Misses Fitz-Clarence, and we used to ask questions about them, and sometimes we read the French letters they wrote to him as exercises, and which he brought away to correct. I remember one passage in those letters, wherein the writer begs to be excused for a very short letter, because she is writing in her father's sick-room, and she is afraid the scratching of her pen will disturb him. These juvenile productions gave us an insight into the domestic life of the retired actress; we could but admire her well-regulated household, and we saw what a good mother she was to her numerous children, who all grew up to be fine men and women. The boys were put into the army and navy, and the girls made grand matches, which, however, they could never have done if their mother had not been so basely used by their father that she felt obliged to quit his roof.

Mrs. Jordan had lived so long with the Duke, and had been so faithful to him, that she felt as if she were legally wedded to him. What, then, must have been her dismay and indignation, when she saw in the newspapers an account of his being a candidate for the hand of the wealthiest heiress in England, Miss Tilnay Long Wellesley Pole! She would not have believed it, if the whole correspondence had not been given. There was the offer of the man whom she considered her husband, and the lady's refusal..

Many women, in her position, would have swallowed the insult, and kept her place at the head of such an establishment; but on finding that the tie which she had considered sacred was contemned by the Duke, she left his roof and went forth penniless, to earn her living by her former profession. It was this spirited action of Mrs. Jordan, and the shameful conduct of the Duke, which gave her such popularity on her reappearance at Covent Garden Theatre. Every expression in the plays she acted, which could be made to apply to her situation, brought down the house and showed John Bull's strong sense of injustice. But this could not last long. She was no longer young; she was enormously fat, and this spoiled her for a comic actress, so she was obliged to leave the stage, and all I know of her, after this, is, that she died in France, so poor as to have a pauper's funeral.

How her children could suffer this, if they knew of her poverty, I cannot imagine; perhaps her disinterested love for them made her keep them ignorant of her whereabouts and her necessities. She may have acted the part of the fabled pelican, and sacrificed herself for the good of her young. If so, she had some reward, even in this life, for her leaving them entirely changed their position in the world. They were immediately noticed by the royal family, received at court, and sought in marriage by the highest nobility.

CHAPTER XII.

BATH. — BEAU NASH. — THE B—— FAMILY.

THOUGH separated by a week's journey from our London friends, we had frequent opportunities of meeting. They would come to see us in Wales, and we would visit them in the metropolis. Sometimes we spent a few weeks in the city of Bath, which was rather more than half-way to London, and there we were sure to meet some of our dearest friends, who made a point of drinking the chalybeate waters there every winter. Bath was then unlike every other city; it was built for the benefit of invalids, who came there on account of the hot mineral springs, and the municipal arrangements were made with regard to them.

Many of the streets were paved all over with large flag-stones, over which no carriages were allowed to pass. There were several hundred sedan chairs, carried by tall porters, dressed in uniform, which were numbered and registered at an office, and obliged to be kept exquisitely clean; numerous rules were made to regulate the behavior and the fares of the chairmen. Wheel-chairs, too, were on the same footing. Very large public baths were maintained by the city for the use of the sick. In the centre, the boiling hot springs bubbled up, and all around the sides were the dressing-rooms for the bathers, who frequently spent hours in the bath, which was shallow enough on one side to admit of stone benches, on which to sit with the water up to the neck. I have seen a man so crippled by rheumatism as to be carried into the bath, and after he had been in a few minutes, he could walk about. All the bathers wore dresses, and men and women went in together.

One great amusement of Bath was the Pump-room, an immense hall with an arched roof. There was a gallery at one end for the band to play in, and at the side, opposite the main entrance, was a marble counter, enclosing the faucets that supplied the company with the mineral waters, and a woman who filled and refilled the glasses. Between each draught, the invalid was ordered to walk half an hour, and those under this treatment took the waters before breakfast and before dinner, and walked up and down the room between each glass. Before breakfast they were without music and without lookers-on; but from two till four o'clock the band played and the room was full, being frequented by many besides the invalids. It was a very gay scene; all the fashion and beauty of the season met there, to walk and talk, to discuss the news of the day and make arrangements for the evening amusements. Two sets of very handsome assembly rooms were provided by the city, and subscription balls were held in them every week. Here, too, the authorities interfered for the good of the invalid: no dancing was allowed after eleven o'clock, and this made people willing to begin at eight. Besides all these peculiar arrangements, there was one still more uncommon, and that was the appointment of a Master of Ceremonies, who continued from year to year to preside over these balls, and did all in his power to promote the pleasure of the visitors. On arriving in Bath, the head of the family was expected to call on the Master of Ceremonies, and leave his card and a guinea fee. Then this call was returned, and all the members of the family were introduced. One man distinguished himself in this walk of life, and made his very equivocal calling to be respected. Beau Nash, as he was called, was a handsome man, with elegant manners, and sufficient confidence in himself not to be put down by the insolence of fashion. He was often ill-treated, and sometimes insulted; but he never appeared to be disturbed by it. He presided over the balls, and was bound to find partners for all the young ladies whose fathers had called on him. This was no easy task, when the exquisites of the day voted dancing to be a bore. He was one evening trying to persuade a knot of young men to take partners, and praising the young girls who wanted to dance, when one of them said, "Very well, Nash; trot 'em by, and let us see them."

One ball, near the beginning of the season, was made more elegant than any other; certain things were required, even in the dress of the ladies; and the ball opened with the stately and graceful dance called the *Minuet de la Cour*, performed by the Master of Ceremonies with any young lady who was coming out into the world for the first time. If there were several *débutantes*, he danced with each, and that was called *coming out*.

It had been fashionable to wear lace aprons in full dress, and all sorts of muslin aprons at other times; but they were no longer the mode, and they were forbidden at this ball. A very fashionable Duchess was about to enter the room with a beautiful point-lace apron on. The doorkeeper told her she could not go in with that apron. She insisted she would, but the man would not permit it; so she sent for Mr. Nash, saying she knew he would not object to such an apron as that. He came, and he did object so strongly that the Duchess was obliged to submit; so she took off the offending lace, and very good-naturedly threw it at Mr. Nash, saying, "There!

take that for your pains." It was a gift of great value, and he returned it the next morning; but she sent it back, saying she meant him to keep it.

On a lady's behaving very rudely to him, he said, "Madam, what do you take me for?" "I take you for the very last link in the scale of gentility." Such cuts as these were hard to bear, but he took them very philosophically. The city authorities were so grateful for his services, that they put up a full-length picture of him in the Pump-room. It happened to be placed between two busts, one of Sir Isaac Newton, the other of some distinguished man, I forget who; but a wit wrote these lines on seeing them:

> "This picture, placed those busts between,
> Gives satire all its strength;
> Wisdom and worth are little seen,
> But folly at full length."

One family, in the habit of going every year to Bath, failed to meet us there; and as their detention at home was occasioned by some curious circumstances, I will relate them here. Mr. B—— was a wealthy merchant of London, and the happy father of eleven children, when he lost his lovely and exemplary wife. A dear friend of hers had become the governess of her children, and on her death-bed she enjoined it on her husband never to part from Miss H——. His eldest daughter, though only eleven years old, took the head of his table, and, with the help of their good old housekeeper, she acted as mistress of the house. When she grew up, her father removed his family to a magnificent country seat in one of the most beautiful counties of England, and she enjoyed organizing the establishment on a large scale. With plenty of good servants, her housekeeping was nothing but a pleasure to her; and she was so happy as the mistress of her father's house, that she refused numerous proposals of marriage, and remained single to a mature age. Her sisters grew up and married, and the governess was no longer needed in the family; but Mr. B—— remembered his wife's injunction, and would not part from her. It was evident that she had become essential to the happiness of their father. When ill, no one was allowed to nurse him but Miss H——; when well, she was his companion; and after tea, which she always poured out, she spent the evening with him in his library, and the young folks saw no more of them that night.

On the occasion of one of the younger daughters being married, a very large family party was assembled under Mr. B——'s roof. They had been several days collecting, and he had been more than usual among them, owing to his companion, Miss H——, being absent on a visit to a widowed brother with a large family of children.

The very night before the wedding, Mr. B—— received a letter from that brother, saying that he had great need of the presence of his sister, and, as she could no longer be necessary to Mr. B——'s children, he wished her to remain with him. This she refused to do in such a manner as led him to suspect that she was secretly married, and, if that were the case, he would never let her leave his roof but as the acknowledged wife of Mr. B——. Thunderstruck by the contents of this letter, he sent for his eldest daughter, and laid it before her. She read it, and said, "Of course Miss H—— is more needed there than here, and you will consent to her living with her brother." "I cannot," faltered out the father, "for I have been married to her twelve years."

Miss B—— sank upon a sofa, and nearly fainted. That proud man, who had always governed his family with an iron rule, now humbled himself to his child, and begged her to forgive him for what he had done. He assured her that it was his consideration for her that made him conceal his marriage. He expected her to accept one of her many offers, and when she left his house for her own, he meant to place his wife at the head of his establishment.

When Miss B—— had sufficiently recovered from the shock of this discovery, she assured her father that none of his children would have objected to his marrying whom he pleased, but they could never cease to regret his having led such a life of deception and concealment. He acknowledged his error, and expressed great contrition, and asked her what he must now do. She requested him to keep his secret till after the wedding, the next morning; and when the bride and groom were off on their wedding tour, he could tell it to all his other children, and then set off in his own carriage, and bring his wife home. "She will not take your place, my dear child; you must still be the mistress of the house." "No, father, that cannot be; she must take the place that belongs to her as your wife. Now, let me go back to my company, and let them perceive nothing of what has happened." She returned to the drawing-room, but such a change had come over her fine face, that her brothers came to her, one after the other, to ask what was the matter. She said she would tell them the next day, and begged them not to ask any questions now.

All the arrangements of the wedding rested on her shoulders, and she went through with it well, notwithstanding the painful secret that lay so heavy at her heart, and the married pair went off quite unconscious that anything remarkable had occurred at home.

All the brothers and sisters were requested to remain a few hours after the wedding was over; and when reassembled in the drawing-room, that unhappy father entered, as a culprit before his children, and disclosed to them his marriage, calling upon his eldest son as a witness of the ceremony. This was an added surprise, but left no doubt on their minds as to the validity of the marriage. That son now came forward to reconcile the children to their father, and make him feel more comfortable before them. He encouraged him to start at once for D——, and to bring his wife home, whilst they were all there to receive her, and install her as mistress of the house. Mr. B——'s daughters had often been made uneasy by observing the great intimacy of their father and Miss H——, and the servants thought so ill of it as to treat her with disrespect. Miss B—— had often consulted her eldest brother about it, and asked him to persuade his father to let Miss H—— depart; but he made light of his sister's alarms, and thought Miss H—— had better stay; the old gentleman needed her care when ill, and her company when well. The seeming indifference of this brother to what pained her so much, always puzzled Miss B——; but now all was explained, and though she felt like a sovereign queen about to abdicate, she was relieved of many old annoyances. She wished her brother to tell the servants what had happened, but he thought she would do it best, as it was she who was about to give up the reins of government. So she assembled them, fifteen in number, in the housekeeper's room, and, having told the facts of the case, she exhorted them to treat with respect and obedience the lawful wife of their master.

The next evening their father would return with his wife. Just before he arrived, Miss B—— took a turn on a terrace-walk behind the house, to cool her head and draw a long breath ; but she was driven back into the house by the sound of the church bells in the village, ringing out a merry peal, in honor of the married pair, as they drove through it. The carriage drove up to the door, and the eldest son handed out Mrs. B——, saluted her kindly, and conducted her into the room where all the relations awaited her. She was overcome to tears, but gratefully received their welcome, and the kisses usually bestowed on her after an absence.

Miss B—— went abroad for six months, and in that time Mrs. B—— became thoroughly initiated into her new position, and did the honors of her house admirably. The neighboring gentry called upon her, and the married sons and daughters, with their children, visited there as much as ever, and were as well received.

Miss B—— told me, that on her return to the paternal mansion, she felt as if she had been dead and was alive again, and found her place entirely filled up.

CHAPTER XIII.

IRELAND. — SIR HARRY BROWN HAYES. — BRENAN.

WHEN I was a girl in my teens, my parents took me with them for a tour in Ireland. The beautiful scenery, the wit and humor of the lower classes, and the hospitality and kindness which we received, made our tour a succession of delightful visits, whilst the peculiar customs of the people, and thrilling narratives of those who had suffered in the late rebellion, amused and interested us much. No good hotel, nor decent road-side inn, was to be found anywhere, except in Dublin. The nobility and gentry expected to entertain all respectable travellers, and were glad to do so, for the sake of their company. We therefore went from one country-seat to another, escorted by part of each family we left to that we were going to, and by the time that we reached the Lakes of Killarney, our party of three was augmented to thirteen. There we experienced the miseries of a bad inn ; and there we learned that it was considered necessary to look after the safety of a young lady, as abduction was the fashion of the day. My room must be inside that of my parents, with no door but that between the two rooms, and the window must be securely fastened. We were told that there was a club of young men who were sworn to assist one another in carrying off any girl they fancied.

It was hard for us to believe this, and my father treated it as a joke upon travellers, until we were visiting an old friend of his, Mr. Penrose, and learned from him that his niece had been carried off, by a stratagem, from the very house we were then in. He gave us the following account of it. Miss Penrose was on a visit to her uncle, whose residence was several miles from that of her mother. One evening, about dusk, a carriage drove up to the door, and a note was sent in to Miss Penrose, informing her that her mother was suddenly taken ill, and had sent a carriage to bring her home. She did not know the equipage or the coachman, but supposed they were hired for the occasion, and went off in it, nothing doubting. Absorbed by the news of her mother's illness, and prevented by the shades of night from observing the road, she had proceeded several miles before she remarked that it was very rough, and that she saw no familiar objects. She called to the coachman, said that he had mistaken the road, and must turn back and find the right one. He pulled up, and the carriage was at once surrounded by men on horseback, one of whom dismounted, entered the carriage, seated himself beside her, and ordered the coachman to drive on.

Astonished beyond all power of expression, she drew back amazed, unable in the twilight to read the face of the intruder. He endeavored to convince her that she was safe under his protection, that he was very much in love with her, and intended honorable marriage. He introduced himself as Sir Henry Brown Hayes, and said he was carrying her to his country-seat, where a clergyman would be in readiness to marry them at once. He ran on in this strain very volubly till they reached his castle, but she hardly heard what he said; she thought only how she could escape from his power. She attempted to let down the glass and scream, but he would not let her do that, and he assured her it would be in vain, for they were far from any human habitation but his own, where they would soon arrive.

She was received with obsequious civility by the housekeeper, whom she saw at once to be the willing instrument of her master's iniquity. Sir Henry led her into a dining-room, where a supper was prepared, and soon half a dozen young men, one of whom had a clerical appearance, followed her into the room. She scanned their faces, but found no hope for her in any of them. Sir Henry acted the gay gallant. He would have the marriage first, and then the wedding feast. Miss Penrose found strength enough to protest against his doings, to declare she would never marry him, and to appeal to the honor of the men around her. It was all in vain; her distress was met only by coarse jokes, and assurances that they were sworn to assist Sir Harry in carrying her off, and marrying her. They made her stand up before the clergyman or priest, I forget which it was. He asked for the ring, and said he could not marry without it. Sir Harry had not provided one, but he took that of his housekeeper, and the wedding service was begun. Miss Penrose caught at the idea that there could be no marriage without a ring, and when Sir Henry was about to put it on her finger, she seized and broke it in two, throwing the fragments away with an air of triumph which provoked Sir Harry, but was laughed at by his companions. He despatched a messenger on horseback, in search of another ring, and then all sat down to supper. Even their unhappy captive ate all she could, by way of keeping up her strength and courage; but she would drink nothing but water, for fear of being drugged. When allowed to retire for the night, she was locked into her room; but she piled up before the door all the furniture she could move. What her feelings and reflections were that night, we never learned; but the next morning, before the messenger arrived with the ring, her friends came to her rescue, and with sufficient force to capture and carry off to jail Sir Henry and two of his accomplices.

Miss Penrose was an heiress, and her abduction made a great sensation throughout the country. Her courage and presence of mind were highly praised, and she was the heroine of the day; but she was of a modest and retiring disposition, and shrank from all notoriety. She dreaded appearing in court, as she knew she must, when the trial of Sir Henry Brown Hayes came on.

He had powerful friends, and the trial was delayed in order to give time for his beard to grow, as he hoped, by disguising himself, to prevent his being identified by Miss Penrose. He not only changed his own appearance so entirely that his best friend did not know him, but he made one of his accomplices, who resembled him in size and complexion, wear the same clothes that he did when he ran away with the heiress, and simulate him as much as possible. At last the trial came on. The court was crammed full, and Miss Penrose was confronted with the abductor and his accomplice. A wand was put into her hand, and she was required to lay it on the head of Sir Henry Brown Hayes. She was startled by the change in his appearance; but after looking earnestly at him, she laid the wand on the right head.

He was convicted, and sentenced to be transported to Botany Bay for seven years. Miss Penrose did not long survive this severe trial of her nerves.

Mr. Penrose had a charming residence on the banks of the beautiful river Lee, six miles above its entrance into the Bay of Cork, and not far from the city. He had a spacious stone house, with ample grounds around it, extensive stables and carriage-house, but all in a dilapidated state; yet at that very time he was building a picture and sculpture gallery. Such were the inconsistencies often seen in Ireland. The inside of the house had not been repaired or painted for many years, the banister of the principal staircase was falling to pieces, and one of the family said, as we came down among the *débris*, "I am afraid you are thinking of *Castle Rackrent*," and so indeed we were.

Another interesting event in our Irish tour, was passing over a mountain, near Cashel, which was infested by a famous highwayman named Brenan, who was represented as such a hero of romance, that I rather hoped we might be robbed by him. He was a deserter from the English army, and his life depended on his keeping out of reach of the clutches of the law. He lived, with his wife, at the foot of a mountain, over which passed the high road, and every part of which was so well known to him that he could hide himself in places inaccessible to his pursuers. Soldiers and civilians were always endeavoring to catch him.

One traveller armed himself with a blunderbus, and swore he would not be robbed by Brenan, but if attacked by him, he would bring him, dead or alive, to Cashel. He was in a post-chaise with the windows all open, and the blunderbus stood in a corner before him. He was on the mountain road frequented by Brenan, and looking out earnestly for him on one side of the road, when a hand on the other side seized his blunderbus, and aimed it at him. Brenan ordered him to throw his pistols and his purse out of the window, or he was a dead man. The traveller obeyed, and then the highwayman said to him, "Now go to Cashel, and tell your friends that though you came out expressly to shoot poor Brenan, he has spared your life."

Two young men, out shooting wild-fowl, met Brenan in the garb of a laborer, but suspected who he was, and told him to walk before them into Cashel, or they would shoot him. After a little remonstrance, and trying to convince them he was not Brenan, he did as he was bid. His fate now seemed certain, but his wife's cleverness saved him. She saw from a distance his danger, and putting a pair of loaded pistols into a basket, and covering them over with a white cloth, as if it were butter or cheese she was carrying to market, she met her husband. He said, "Hullo, Goody, what have you got to sell?" seized his pistols, and being close to his enemies, he put the muzzles to their breasts, and told them to throw down their guns, and his wife fired them off. "Go," said Brenan, "and tell your friends that Brenan has a good wife." She saved him once when he was caught in bed, by clinging to his pursuer, whilst he ran off. He never enriched himself, but made friends of the poor, by bestowing on them the money he took from the wealthy. He was at last taken by a regiment of soldiers being distributed around the base of the mountain which he frequented, and marching up its sides, closing ranks as they went. He retreated to the top, and buried himself under a pile of furze; suspecting he was there, but not liking to handle such prickly stuff, they thrust their bayonets into it, and he received numerous stabs before he called out and surrendered.

Some noble traits in Brenan had interested a member of Parliament in his favor, and he was negotiating with those in authority for his pardon, and for liberty to join the English army then fighting the French in Spain; but before this could be arranged, the poor fellow was executed as a highway robber.

My father had visited Ireland in 1797, before

the rebellion broke out there, and had felt much pity for the unhappy peasantry of that country. He thought the measures of the English government were cruel and unjust in the extreme. Being a guest at one of the viceroy's grand dinners, the state of Ireland was discussed in a manner very distasteful to him, and he was called upon, as an impartial spectator, to give his opinions, which he declined doing; but, on being urged to do so by Lord Camden (the viceroy), he said he would be happy to talk with him on the state of Ireland, if he would give him a private interview. This the Earl agreed to do, and a time was named for it. My father had not grown up in America without imbibing ideas of justice and liberty, which were outraged by the treatment which the Irish were receiving at the hands of the English civil and military authorities, and he spoke out his mind fully and fearlessly to Lord Camden, a most narrow-minded old Tory. When my father said that the conduct of the military was enough to drive the people into rebellion, the Viceroy replied, that was exactly what they wished to do; they wished to bring matters to a crisis, and then they could deal with it peremptorily. "If that is your policy," said my father, "you are certainly taking the right means to accomplish your purpose"; and with these words he closed the interview. The rebellion broke out soon after, and proved a scene of bloodshed and cruelty on both sides fearful to hear of. Our visit to Ireland was ten years after the conclusion of that terrible civil war, and though it only lasted eight weeks, the country was but just recovering from its consequences, and every family had its tragic story to tell of peril and suffering. My father was never tired of hearing them, but they harrowed up my feelings so much that I rather avoided them, and have but few laid up in my mind. I do, however, remember being at a country residence, where one of the family, a girl of my own age, told me that her parents narrowly escaped assassination by the defeat of the rebels in a fight near their place. A man servant, who had faithfully served them many years, was observed to be much disturbed; he was seen shedding tears, and going continually to the gate, at the end of their avenue, to look out for news from some passer by. When questioned, he would not tell what troubled him; but before night, news came of the defeat of the rebels, and then he cried for joy, and told his master that he knew of the impending battle, and that the rebel leader intended, if victorious, to come there and murder the family and take possession of the house. When asked why he did not warn them of their danger, he said he could not, without breaking his oath as a *United Irishman.*

I also remember being shown a man who had been dead and buried three days, but came to life again, and told me his own story. He was a loyal man of Eniscorthy, and wandered heedlessly into the camp of the rebels, on a height called Vinegar Hill, near the town. He was shot by a sentry for not having the countersign, his body was thrown into an old ruined windmill, and a little earth thrown over it. His wife, hearing he was killed, sent a request for his body by an idiot well known in the town. Being refused, she then went herself, taking the idiot with her to help carry her dead husband. She succeeded, after much importunity, in getting possession of the body, and carrying it home. As they took him up a narrow winding stairway, his wound pained him, and he uttered a groan, which so frightened them that they let him fall, and that shock revived him. His wound was dressed, and he recovered to tell the story to every one who would listen to it.

CHAPTER XIV.

MISS EDGEWORTH.

MY last chapter on Ireland recalls another tour in that country, made with my hus band, twenty years later in my life. We arrived in Dublin, accompanied by a young friend, and sent off our letter of introduction to Miss Edgeworth, with one from me proposing to spend a day with her, if convenient and agreeable. To this we received the following very gracious reply: —

EDGEWORTHTOWN, September 3, 1836.

DEAR MADAM: — I hasten to assure you and Professor Farrar that we feel highly honored and gratified by your kind intention of paying us a visit. Mrs. Edgeworth desires me to say, that we shall be at home all next week, and we shall be most happy to receive you, and your young friend Mr. W——, any day after the fifth which may be most convenient to you. We say after the fifth, because on the fifth my sister (Harriet), Mrs. Butler, and her husband, the Rev. Mr. Butler, will come to us, and independently of the pleasure they will have, I am sure, in your society, I own I wish that you should become acquainted with them, especially as we are unlucky at this moment, in not having any of my brothers at home. My brother-in-law, Mr. Butler, is, as you will find, a man of literature and learning, besides being all that you will like in other respects, from the truth and rectitude and simplicity of his character.

I am much obliged to you for the letters you were so good as to enclose to me. Of all our friends in Boston and Cambridge, we shall, I hope, have time to inquire further and to converse.

There was only one thing in your letter which did not give us pleasure; and we trust that after your arrival, and after you have had some hours to reflect, and a night quietly to sleep upon it, you will repent and recant, and give up your *cruel purpose* of giving us only one day. Mrs. Edgeworth will remonstrate with you, I think, more effectually than I can, and in the mean time I promise to allow you till the morning after your arrival to become sufficiently acquainted with the ways of the house and family, before I turn to you, as I shall (I warn you) at breakfast, for your *ultimatum*.

I am, dear Madam, (for the present,)
Your much obliged and grateful
MARIA EDGEWORTH.

P. S. It must increase my interest in making your acquaintance, my dear Mrs. Farrar, to know that you are sister to Mr. Benjamin Rotch, whose talents I with great reason admire, and for whose kindness and agreeable letters I have equally great reason to be grateful.

The cordiality and frankness of this letter made us all desirous of visiting the writer. We were much struck with the manner in which Mrs. Edgeworth was mentioned and made of importance as the lady of the house, when the whole place was the property of Miss Edgeworth, and she was at least thirty years older than her step-mother. Mr. Edgeworth had been dead several years, and his son had become so embarrassed in his affairs as to be obliged to sell his patrimonial estate; and to prevent its passing into the hands of strangers, Miss Edgeworth had bought it, and made her step-mother mistress of the establishment, whilst she lived with her as a daughter. They were on the very best terms, each admiring and loving the other. Another member of the family was Mrs. Mary Sneyd, a very aged lady of the old school, and sister to Honoria Sneyd, who refused the hand of Major André, and became the wife of Richard Lovel Edgeworth. The unhappy fate of the gallant Major is well known; but few persons now living ever read the monody written on his death by Miss Seward, in which she makes her hero say,

> "Honoria lost, I woo a sterner bride;
> The armed Bellona calls me to her side."

It was a great pleasure to me to see the sister of two of Mr. Edgeworth's wives; one belonging to the same period, and dressed in the same style, as the lovely Honoria. She did not appear till lunch time, when we found her seated at the table, in a wheel-chair, on account of her lameness. She reminded me of the pictures of the court beauties of the time of Louis XIV. Her dress was truly elegant, and very elaborate. Her white hair had the effect of powder, and the structure on it defies description. A very white throat was set off to advantage by a narrow black velvet ribbon, fastened by a jewel. The finest lace ruffles about her neck and elbows, with a long-waisted silk dress of rich texture and delicate color, produced an effect that was quite bewitching. She was wonderfully well preserved for a lady of over eighty years of age, and it was pleasant to see the great attention paid to her by all the family. She was rather deaf, so I was seated by her side, and requested to address my conversation to her. When lunch was over, she was wheeled into the library, and occupied herself making a cotton net to put over the wall-fruit, to keep it from the birds. It was worth a journey to Edgeworthtown only to see this elegant specimen of old age.

I had heard that Mr. Edgeworth's house was full of his inventions and contrivances, and when shown to our bedroom, we found such an extraordinary lock on the door, that we dared not shut it for fear of not being able to open it again. That room, too, was unlike any other I ever saw. It was very large, with three huge windows, two of them heavily curtained, and the third converted into a small wardrobe, with doors of pink cotton on a wooden frame. It had two very large four-posted bedsteads, with full suits of curtains, and an immense folding screen that divided the room in two, making each occupant as private as if in a separate room, with a dressing-table and ample washing conveniences on each side. A large grate, filled with turf, and all ready for lighting, with a great basket lined with tin, and also filled with the same fuel, reminded us strongly we were in Ireland. Large wax candles were on the mantlepiece, and every convenience necessary to our comfort; at the same time the furniture was so very old-fashioned and dilapidated, that no one in this country would think it possible to use it.

We were shown other contrivances of the former owner, such as a door in the entrance hall, (through which the servants were continually passing,) the motion of which wound up a clock, the face being over the sideboard, in the dining-room. Several doors in the house were made double, in a way that I could not see the use of. Two doors were fastened together at the hinge side, making a right angle with each other, so that in opening one door you shut the other, and had to open that before you could enter, and when that opened, the one behind you shut. Miss Edgeworth said it was for safety in times of danger. She always mentioned her father with great respect, and even reverence, in her manner; but nothing that I saw or heard there raised my opinion of him. I think his never allowing his gifted daughter any retirement, but insisting on her writing all her books in that great library, where he was teaching the children their lessons, and every one occupied in various ways, was a real act of tyranny, but she did not so regard it.

In building his house, Mr. Edgeworth would have no drawing-room, no sitting-room but the one large library, with numerous windows on one side, some made into alcoves by projecting book-shelves. There were a great many books, some fine engravings, beautiful drawings, and very good oil paintings by Mrs. Edgeworth. It was a very pleasant family room, fully furnished with tables, sofas, and lounges, a curious clock, and various models. A little old fashioned work-table, with a small desk on it, was used by Miss Edgeworth for writing all her books.

The fourth wife of Mr. Edgeworth was our hostess, and performed her part charmingly. She must have been very pretty, for, though short, fat, and forty, her appearance was very agreeable. Miss Edgeworth was shorter still, and carried herself very upright, with a dapper figure and quick movements. She was the remains of a blonde, with light eyes and hair; she was now gray, but wore a dark frizette, whilst the gray hair showed through her cap behind. She was so plain that she was never willing to sit for her portrait, and that is the reason why the public has never been made acquainted with her personal appearance.

In conversation we found her delightful. She was full of anecdotes about remarkable people, and often spoke from her personal knowledge of them. Her memory, too, was stored with valuable information, and her manner of narrating was so animated, that it was difficult to realize her age. In telling an anecdote of Mirabeau, she stepped out before us, and extending her arm, spoke a sentence of his in the impassioned manner of a French orator, and did it so admirably that it was quite thrilling.

She told us two speeches of Madame de Staël which are worth remembering. Madame Neckar was a harsh mother, and always found a great deal of fault with her daughter; but her husband knew his child's merits, and liked her to have her own way. One day a gentleman entered the room, just as Madame Neckar flourished out of it, after reprimanding her daughter, who stood abashed in the middle of the room, with tears on her face. He endeavored to console her by saying that she must not mind her mother's reproofs, as long as her father was satisfied with her, and he told her how much Mr. Neckar admired her. To this the girl replied, "*Mon père pense à mon bonheur present, ma mère songe à mon avenir.*" I talked with Miss Edgeworth of a work on Progressive Education by Madame Neckar de Saussure; she thought it dull and tedious, and said that Madame de Staël had a great admiration of that cousin, and said of her, "*Elle a tous les talens qu' on me suppose, et toutes les vertues qui me manquent.*"

Miss Edgeworth and all her family took the part of the English Government in their treatment of the Irish, and had no sympathy for the wrongs and sufferings of their countrymen. Bigoted Episcopalians, they would grant no rights to the Roman Catholics, and this made them very unpopular in their own neighborhood.

They had been instrumental in establishing a free school for the sons of poor Protestant clergymen, in the town which bordered on their grounds, and they took us to see it. It was market-day, so the main street was full of the lower order of Irish, with their horses and carts, asses and panniers, tables and stands full of eatables and articles of clothing. Sometimes the cart, or car, served as a counter on which to display their goods. The women in gay-colored cotton gowns, and white caps with full double borders, made a very gay appearance. As we all passed through the crowd to the school-house, the enmity of the Papists to Protestant landholders was but too evident.

Though Mrs. Edgeworth had been the Lady Bountiful of the village for many years, there were no bows or smirks for her and her friends, no making way before her, no touching of hats or pleasant looks. A sullen expression and a dogged immovability were on every side of us. Mr. Butler, who had but just arrived in Edgeworthtown, was as much struck with it as we were, and it quite excited him. He spoke of it to us as a want of manners in the people, and called them uncivilized; but there was more in it than that. He spoke to us Americans of the long train of oppressive measures under which the Irish had groaned for years; of the Protestant clergy paid by rates levied on the Roman

Catholics, and of the tyranny exercised by Protestant landholders. Twenty-eight years have passed since I stood in that Irish crowd, and much has been done to improve their condition; all the political disabilities then complained of by the Papists have been removed, oppressive laws have been done away with, emigration has relieved the land of its surplus population, and were it not for the designs of the Romish Church to rescue the island from the dominion of a Protestant power, that country might now be prosperous and happy.

When we visited Miss Edgeworth she had published her last work, "Helen," and was writing another to be called "Taking for Granted," but I never heard of its being published. She told me that she meant to show the mischief of taking things for granted, and acting upon them as if they were known facts, and she begged me to send her any instances of the evil consequences of "taking for granted" which fell under my observation.

CHAPTER XV.

ANDRIANE.

I HAPPENED to be in Paris in 1737 when Monsieur Andriane returned from his ten years' imprisonment in Austrian dungeons, and I was present in the saloon of Madame Récamier, when he gave a most affecting account of his sufferings. He was in the prime of life, and had been handsome, but he was prematurely aged by all he had endured. His sight was much impaired by writing on the walls of his dungeon with scarcely any light, and he was lamed for life by the heavy irons he had worn so many years. I can see him now as he was seated in the centre of a circle of eager listeners, answering questions, and describing with great pathos the effect on his mind of the solitary imprisonment which he endured for a part of the time. He was a young Frenchman travelling for pleasure, and had had nothing to do with the politics of Europe. On leaving Geneva to go to Milan, a friend asked him to be the bearer of some papers which he wished to send to that city. Entirely ignorant of their being the communications of a secret society, plotting against the Austrian government, he took charge of them. On his way over the Simplon, his carriage was upset, and many of its contents fell over the precipice at the side of the road, and among them the portfolio containing those dangerous papers. His servant insisted on going down the precipice after his master's effects, and when all but the portfolio were recovered, Monsieur Andriane begged him not to risk his life for that, but the man's zeal to serve him made him bring that up also. The fatal papers arrived at Milan, and before the bearer had time to deliver them, they were in the hands of the police, and he was arrested. His astonishment was unbounded, and in his first examination it was difficult to make him understand what he had done to forfeit his liberty, or of what he was accused, but he had enough presence of mind to refuse to tell who had given him the papers, or to whom they were to be delivered. This reserve made him appear to belong to the secret society then existing in Milan, and he was therefore considered as plotting against the Austrian government, and condemned to the severest imprisonment.

As soon as he was supposed sufficiently broken down to be willing to betray his associates, for the sake of better treatment, he was subjected to another examination; but they had mistaken their man. His sense of honor never failed him, and during ten years of persecution, he never yielded to persuasion, threats, or bribery, but steadily refused to give any information which could compromise anybody. He suffered accordingly all the cruelties inflicted on suspected persons. He was asked how he employed his mind during his solitary confinement, and told us that for the first year he went over his past life, recalling every minute circumstance, and kept his mind busy; after that he felt that he was becoming stupid, and fearing to be imbecile, he roused himself to fresh exertion, and began to recall all that he had ever learned from books, and wrote it on the wall with the point of a rusty old nail that he found in his cell. It was only during the middle of the day that the faint light which entered his dungeon was sufficient for him to pursue this occupation, but he found it very useful, and a great alleviation. During the many hours of darkness, he would recall and prepare what he would write the next day. He feared that in a long imprisonment his memory might fail him, and then he hoped the writing on the wall would save him from imbecility. He had completely covered all his walls, as high as he could reach, with fine writing, when he was suddenly removed to another dungeon. This was done, he supposed, on purpose to torment him; but it proved a blessing, for he began again, arranged his matter better, beginning with his spelling book and grammar, and continuing all through his classical education, he wrote down every word he could remember.

The prison became so full that it was necessary to put two in each dungeon, and Andriane had the immense advantage of being associated with that excellent man, Gonfalonieri. He could not enlarge on the blessed effects of that fellowship. It occasioned him too much emotion, and he hastened to the end of his narrative, by saying that great exertions were made by his friends to procure his liberty, but in vain. The officials hated him for his obstinate refusals to answer certain questions, and when they found how much he enjoyed the society of the noble Gonfalonieri, they changed his companion for a very degraded felon. This was his greatest trial, but he said, "Gonfaloneri had taught me how to bear even that." He ended by saying, "I owe my liberty at last to the perseverance of this dear sister," and he laid his hand in the lap of a lady who was sitting almost behind him, and nearly hidden from our view. The sister now became an object of interest to the company, and after some conversation with her the party broke up.

I never saw or heard anything of Monsieur Andriane for more than twenty years, when I found myself living under the same roof with him and his family at Pau, in the south of France. He was now happily married, and had one son, nearly of age, and a young daughter. They were all skilled in music, and the son always played the accompaniments to his mother's singing, which was remarkably fine. They had musical parties every other week, to which the *beau monde* of Pau thought it a great favor to be invited. The misfortunes of Andriane's youth had taught him to prize very highly his present happiness; he still bears about him the ill effects of his long imprisonment, and he always kept the anniversary of his release from prison as a sacred day. It occurred whilst I was at Pau, and I sent him a handsome bouquet, with a few lines of congratulation on his present happiness. I never saw a person more delighted with a slight attention than he was with mine. He called the next day to thank me, and was so profuse in his acknowledgments that I was convinced his more fashionable friends had not noticed the day.

CHAPTER XVI.

THE FRENCH STAGE.

IT was my good fortune to be in Paris just in time to see Talma and Mlle. Georges perform their best characters in the plays of Racine, before leaving the stage. The scene which has left the most vivid impression on my mind is one in the play of Britannicus, where Agrippina is reproaching Nero with his faults in a fearless and authoritative manner, whilst he is chafing with suppressed rage. The perfection of their costume, and the excellence of their acting, made me feel as though I had seen the real personages they were simulating. I preferred Talma's style of acting to that of the Kemble school; for, though his style was not less "classical," it had more of nature in it. Though every word and movement of Talma was studied and finished to the last degree of perfection, he was less conventional than John Kemble.

Talma's figure reminded me of that of Napoleon, and I can well believe that the latter took lessons from the great tragedian, and learned of him how best to carry his robes of state. Why should not one actor learn of another?

Twenty years later, I was again in Paris, and again frequented that best of theatres, which is subsidized by the government, and is called emphatically *Le Théatre François.* Napoleon's favorite actress, Mlle. Mars, was still attracting crowds to see her play in the small pieces, written expressly for her, two of which were given on one night. She was no longer young, and many considered her quite *passée;* but on the stage, she still appeared in the prime of life, and her charming acting, elegant carriage, and perfect rendering of her part, made her still the idol of the public.

I saw her in *Marie ou les Trois Époques.* In the first epoch she appears as a young girl, in love with one person, and obliged to marry another, to save her father from ruin. In the next she appears as the faithful and devoted wife, refusing all attentions and all intimacy with her former lover, though her husband, ignorant of the love that once existed between them, is continually throwing them together. He proposes to take a long journey, and leave the *quondam* lover to take care of his wife. This, she positively refuses, and insists on accompanying her husband. Thus ends the second epoch. In the third, she is the mother of a grown-up and beautiful daughter; her husband is dead, and her former lover is continually at her house, and appears to be devoted to her. She remarks with pleasure that her daughter seems very fond of her future step-father; but when asked for a private interview, and expecting to be solicited to marry him, she finds that it is her daughter whom he wants as his wife; and she resigns herself to her fate, with the same disinterestedness that has marked her whole course of life.

Mlle. Mars contrived to look young enough for the first epoch, and won all hearts by the way in which she resigned her lover to save her father from bankruptcy. As the wife, her behavior to her husband was perfect, and might have served as a lesson in morals to French wives. As the mother, nobly preferring her child's happiness to her own, she melted us to pity and sorrow, that such a second sacrifice was required of her.

It was a charming little play, and charmingly performed, and made such an impression on my mind that I can recall it vividly after a lapse of twenty-seven years.

I also saw Mlle. Mars in *Valérie*, — a blind girl who is restored to sight by her lover, — but I do not remember the particulars of the story, only that it was well performed and a very good piece. It would be just the drama for private theatricals where there were but few performers.

Two pieces, in which Mlle. Mars did not act, made a strong impression on me, as showing a great change in the policy of the French government since my previous visit to Paris. Then Louis XVIII. was on the throne: now Louis Philippe was king of the French. One of these remarkable dramas was called *La Viellesse d'un Grand Roi*, in which Louis XIV. is represented at the close of life, almost imbecile, and managed and imposed upon by Madame de Maintenon. How one of the house of Bourbon could permit *le grand Monarque* to be shown up in such a contemptible plight, I never could comprehend. The courtiers were represented as deceiving and making fun of the poor old king, and the audience sympathized with them.

I was equally surprised by the acting of another piece, which favored Protestantism and condemned the practices of the Romish Church. It was written by Scribe, and called *La Famille du temps de Luther*. It represented a young man, just converted to Protestantism, on the point of making a profession of it, and joining a Lutheran church, when his brother arrives from Rome expressly to save him from such damning heresy. They have conversations together, which were entirely favorable to Protestantism, and betrayed the bad morals of the Roman Catholic brother, who is a Jesuit. He uses every means to save his brother from joining the Protestant Church, and considers his soul is safe until that act is performed. So, when bribes and menaces have failed, he resolves to murder him, in order to save his soul from perdition. In his soliloquy before the deed, he expresses that dangerous maxim of the Church of Rome, that *the end justifies the means.* Very different is the soliloquy of the Lutheran brother, the night before he is to make his profession of faith. He speaks as a truly devout man, and a convert to the religion of Christ, before it was corrupted by the Church of Rome. He shows himself so true a Christian, that we feel that he is fit to die, as he does, by the hand of his brother, that night.

It was plain that the audience sympathized with the Protestant brother; and the wonder was how such a piece could be acted in a Roman Catholic country, governed by a Roman Catholic king with a very bigoted wife.

Another great treat which I enjoyed that winter, in Paris, was seeing some of Molière's best comedies at the *Théatre Français*, where every part is sure to be well performed. *L'École des Femmes* was given with a preparatory scene, in which Molière is represented as reading the play to a circle of the *haute noblesse* belonging to the court of Louis XIV. They criticise the piece, and he makes a witty defence. This lasts a short time, and then the circle breaks up, and the critics request Molière to give them the whole play on the stage. It was a very pretty sight to see so many persons, dressed in the costume of those days, and feel assured that they were given correctly.

When we consider the age in which Molière lived, we must award him the merit of having done more honor to the female character than any of his contemporaries. He showed up the evils of mercenary marriages, and was in favor of educating women. The weapon with which he attacked the prevailing follies of the age was ridicule, and he wielded it with a master's hand.

I heard an anecdote of Mlle. Mars, which shows that she was not only the mouth-piece for Molière's wit, but had wit of her own. She was a warm partisan of Napoleon I., and adhered to him during his exile in Elba. The *Garde du Corps* of the Emperor was considered to be mere parade soldiers, and to have no military character at all. Several of them were walking in the gardens of the Tuileries, when they met Mlle. Mars, and made some impertinent remark, on which she said, "*Sachez, Messieurs, que Mars, et le Garde du Corps, n'ont rien de commun ensemble.*" This *bon mot* made her more popular than ever with the Parisians.

During Napoleon's absence in Elba, his friends used the *violet* as his emblem, his countersign, his name. They had a phrase by which to distinguish his partisans. They would say, in a careless way, "*Les violettes reviendront avec le printemps.*" And if the reply was, "*Eh bien!*" they knew they were speaking to a partisan; but if the reply was anything else, the conversation was turned away from the interests of Napoleon.

When he marched triumphantly back to his capital, he showed himself to the people by going to the theatre. Mlle. Mars was playing that night, and had on a dress trimmed with violets.

CHAPTER XVII.

MR. AND MRS. THOMAS HOPE.

THE most brilliant party that I was ever at in London, was given by Mrs. Thomas Hope, the daughter of the Archbishop of Tuam, and wife of the learned author of "Anastatius," a wealthy merchant of Amsterdam resident in London. They lived in a corner house in Harley Street, at the West end of London, and it was large enough to contain fourteen rooms *en suite*. These were fitted up with great taste and judgment, according to the ideas of Mr. Hope, who had written a book on furniture and upholstery, and introduced into England the classical forms which have ever since been in use. This house was like a museum, for every room was fitted up in a different style. One was *à la Chinoise*, and filled with curious and beautiful objects from China; another was in Persian style, full of Eastern magnificence. A Grecian hall, adorned with statuary, delighted the eye, and a French saloon, full of mirrors, with objects of *vertu*, marquetry and *ormolu*, Sèvres porcelain and bronzes, claimed the attention of the visitor. The English apartment, emphatically so called, was the banqueting hall, across one end of which was a long table filled with every delicacy of the season, and where you took refreshments whenever you pleased. There were so many valuable things scattered all through these rooms, that, as I was afterwards told, there was a policeman, dressed as a gentleman, on guard in every room. The fashionables and grandees laughed at the wealthy Dutchman, and called him Furniture Hope; but they were glad enough to throng his house and see his fine collection of paintings and sculpture, nor was his beautiful wife a less attraction. She was so diminutive in her person, and so handsome in her face, that she was called the pocket Venus. The Prince Regent requested her to allow him to have her full-length likeness in enamel, for his collection of beauties; and Mr. Bone, the celebrated painter in enamel, made a lovely picture of her. The night that I saw her, she received her company standing on a low stool, and was dressed in gold-colored satin trimmed with black velvet, and had on a superb set of diamonds.

I went with some particular friends of the Hopes. We had dined at a house only a mile from Mr. Hope's, but it took us two hours to go that distance, in a line of carriages that extended all the way there, and was checked in its progress every time a carriage stopped to set down its company. Directions had been given in the morning papers for the course the carriages were to take, so as to avoid confusion. They were all to approach through the same streets and in the same direction, and after setting down, to proceed through certain other streets, and then fall into line again and approach the house in the same way as before. On reaching Mr. Hope's door, the footman was to give the name of his mistress, and "Mrs. Smith's carriage stops the way!" was vociferated by the servants up the grand staircase to the entrance of the first room, and woe be to Mrs. Smith if she did not hear and attend to the announcement, for her carriage would be ordered to move on, and she must wait till all the company was gone, before she could get it again. I was with friends who knew exactly what to do; so after a few words with the exquisite little hostess, we sauntered slowly through the rooms, all of which were filled but not crowded. We soon came to the large English drawing-room, where we felt "the soft crush of aristocracy," and pressing gently through it, we came suddenly on an open space, in which a large, fat gentleman was bowing to a lady who was just introduced to him. It was the Prince Regent; I knew him by his bow, and we drew back so as not to intrude on the magic circle around royalty. We paused a few minutes to observe him. A once handsome man, bloated and disfigured by dissipation. The lady just introduced was a great wit, and she soon made him shake his fat sides with laughter. On a raised seat, that ran round one half of the room, sat Lady Hertford, his *chère amie* at that time, and very handsome still, though far from young; very stout and tall, with a great display of neck, shoulders, and arms, as fair as alabaster. There she sat, in dignified composure, but watching the Prince. We soon passed on to complete our view of the fourteen rooms. They terminated in an elegant little *boudoir*, where we found only one person, a fashionable dandy of that day. He was standing before a mirror that reflected his whole person, and adjusting his hair and cravat. I knew at once that it was Mr. Skeffington, having seen him mimicked by Mathews the comedian, in his entertainment called "Mathews at Home." As soon as we had completed the tour of the rooms, it was time to place ourselves where we could hear the announcement of our carriage. Standing in the hall at the top of the staircase, we had time to look at a large picture of Belshazzar's Feast, and on our way home I listened to the following account of it.

Mr. Hope bought a great many pictures, and always employed the same man to clean them and put them in order before they were hung. He was on the point of leaving London for his seat in Surrey when the picture of Belshazzar's Feast came into his possession, and he left it with this man to do the needful, and hang it in the hall. On his return to town, he examined the picture, and found that a piece had been cut off the top of it, and the cleaner had put his own name in an obscure part of the picture as the painter of it. Such liberties taken with a valuable picture by an old master, were not to be endured, and the culprit was dismissed with a sharp reprimand. Being something of an artist, he resolved to avenge himself by making a picture of Mr. and Mrs. Hope as *Beauty and the Beast.* Mr. Hope was as ugly as his wife was handsome, and he was represented as the Beast, holding up a full purse to the Beauty. This picture was exhibited as a shilling show, and hundreds flocked to see it before the family knew anything about it. At last a brother of Mrs. Hope, who was an officer in a regiment then on duty at the palace, and therefore wore his uniform, entered the room where this picture was, drew his sword and cut it into strips. The painter sued him for damages, but all he could recover was the price of the canvas and paint!

Mr. Hope, when I knew him, had not published his remarkable novel called "Anastasius"; but, when that appeared, his book on furniture was forgotten, and the public learned to appreciate him as a fine scholar and a good writer. He was very desirous of a son and heir to all his wealth, and three times did his wife present him with a son who died in infancy. The fourth son lived to be five years old. I saw him then, a beautiful boy, the idol of his mother, but I do not know whether he lived to grow up.

CHAPTER XVIII.

THE MISSES ALLEN. — MRS. SISMONDI. — THE YOUNG WIDOW.

THE fathers of families are very apt to hold up, as models of good behavior, some one set of girls whom they wish their daughters to imitate; and when I was growing up, the Miss Allens were the examples always set before me. If I wished to do anything, of which my father disapproved, he would say, "You never heard of one of the Miss Allens doing such a thing as that." When this was said, I knew there was no hope for me, so I resigned myself to be as wise and sober as those pattern girls. They were of an ancient Welch family, and when I knew them, their parents were dead, and they lived with their bachelor brother, a man of mark in the county which he represented in Parliament, and very agreeable in private life. His house was one of our most delightful visiting places. The sisters were better educated and more highly cultivated than was common, at that time, among young ladies in South Wales, and a yearly visit to London introduced them to many distinguished people. One of them married Sir James Mackintosh, two married Wedgwoods, and one was the wife of Sismondi, the historian of Italy.

My husband and I were spending a few weeks in Geneva, in the autumn of 1838, and there I renewed my acquaintance with Mrs. Sismondi, who retained a lively interest in the friend of her youth, and paid us every kind attention. She lived in a villa, a little way out of the town, and received her friends on one evening in every week. To those receptions we always went, and had the most delightful intercourse with her and her accomplished husband, who spoke English well, and had a great respect for republican institutions. He gave us one evening a very interesting account of his flight into Switzerland, with his invalid mother, when obliged, by his liberal opinions, to quit his native land. It so enchained my attention, at the time, that I hardly remarked, among the guests, Mr. Nightingale and his two young daughters. Little did any one then present anticipate the wide-world fame that Miss Florence Nightingale would one day acquire.

We met at Madame Sismondi's the celebrated botanist, M. de Candolle, and by way of making conversation, I told him that in London people were making plants grow under glass shades, shut up tight, without additional air or water.

He listened very incredulously, and made me describe minutely every example of it I had seen. The subject so interested him that in a few days he set off for London to examine into the matter for himself. His absence, at that time, was a disappointment to the Duke of Devonshire, who came to Geneva expressly to talk with him about air-plants, which were then all the rage.

When the loved and respected Miss Allen of Cresselly was first engaged to marry an Italian, her friends trembled for her happiness; but could they have seen her, as I did, after twenty years of married life, they would have been convinced she was blest with a true union, and that she and her Italian husband were as much lovers then as any bride and bridegroom could be. Having no children, they were all the world to each other. The literary labors of the successful author never interfered with his domestic affections. He was full of consideration and tenderness for his wife, and had a most cordial kindness for her friends.

Recalling this visit to Geneva, reminds me of our journey from there to Turin, over Mont Cénis, and of an incident which occurred at San Michele. We arrived early in a fine October evening, and took a walk which brought us unexpectedly to a grand view of Mont Cénis, just as it was brilliantly illuminated by the setting sun. At first several other snowy peaks were equally lighted up, but by degrees all faded but that one, showing how much higher it was than the rest, yet the next day we were to cross its summit. Returning to our inn, which we had left so quiet that it hardly seemed like a public house, we found it all bustle and confusion, and I heard groans and cries from a chamber above our parlor.

On inquiry, we were told that a gentleman and lady, with a maid-servant, had arrived from Turin, and on entering the inn, the lady ran with all speed up stairs and threw herself out of a chamber-window. She broke no bones, but was much hurt and bruised, and it was her groans that I heard. I immediately sent a message to the gentleman offering my services and the use of my medicine-chest. He came to thank me in person, declined my aid, and told me the lady was only twenty-two years of age, the wife of a Brazil merchant who had died suddenly at Naples. As he was Chargé d'Affaires of the Emperor of Brazil, he had been requested to escort this lady as far as Turin, where her friends were to meet him and relieve him of his very unpleasant charge; but no one came, and he should be obliged to go on with her to Geneva, which was very inconvenient and disagreeable to him. Not one word of sympathy or compassion for the distracted widow, nothing but his own disinclination to accompany her, was apparent in his conversation with me. He gave me his own history and his wife's, none of which did I care to hear; my inquiries were only for the unfortunate lady, and of her he did not care to speak. However, I did find out that she was Madame Piton, and that she had not been distracted until to-day, on their way from Turin, and then I surmised that the egotism of this unfeeling man had made him say such hard things about her friends not meeting her there, that it was more than she could bear, added to her deep affliction, and that it was his want of sympathy for her which had driven her to despair and caused her to throw herself from the window. I was disgusted with this Chevalier S. de Macédo, and begged leave to see the lady and to watch with her that night; but he would not let me do either; he thought her maid was sufficient. I sat up late that night, writing my journal, and had not all been silent and still in the poor lady's room before I retired, I should have made an attempt to see her; hoping she was at rest, I went to bed, but it was long before I could sleep for thinking of her.

The next morning we started on our journey over Mont Cénis, before I could hear anything of Madame Piton, and I never expected to hear of her again, but I did. The next spring I was in Paris, and I searched in vain for the lady with whom I had once boarded for six months, and for whom I felt a real friendship. She used to confide to me her troubles, and told me she had been happily married in Marseilles, and as long as she lived there her husband behaved well. He removed to Paris, was well established there in a good business, but he took to gambling, reduced himself to poverty, and then committed some crime which sent him to prison for several years. Meanwhile she supported herself and two sons, and when they were sufficiently educated she meant to leave the country, before her husband was liberated. Not finding her in Paris, I supposed that she had accomplished her purpose. My husband and I went to Rouen on our way to England, and took the steamer on the Seine for our conveyance. On that boat I found my friend Madame Reybert, then on her way to Brazil. She had intended to leave Paris three months sooner, but had been detained by her care of a friend, who had been made insane by grief for the loss of her husband and the total want of sympathy in all around her. I told her of the lady who threw herself out of a window from the same cause. She exclaimed, "That must be my friend, Madame Piton; she did that on her journey with a selfish monster who had no pity for her." Then she gave a moving account of the inhumanity of that man and the indifference of her maid. "I cured her by love and sympathy. One of her delusions was mistaking me for a sister, whom she loved very much, and the happiness which that gave her aided in her recovery. She will return to her mother and sister in Brazil, and there I am going to live near them, for they are old friends of mine." A happy sequel this, to the history of both those ladies!

CHAPTER XIX.

LADY MANSFIELD. — CHILDREN IN A CAVE. — THE HAUNTED HOUSE.

I RECOLLECT a notable instance of the mischief done by a lady's supposing herself to have a head for business, when she really knew nothing about it; and as I have already described the rise and progress of the town of Milford, under the management of the Honorable Charles Greville, I will now tell of its decline and fall under the misrule of Lady Mansfield, whose second husband was the Honorable Robert Fulk Greville, brother of Charles, and heir to his uncle, Sir William Hamilton. Her first husband was the celebrated jurist, Lord Mansfield, who showed what his feelings had been towards her, by giving directions that after his death his heart should be taken out and buried by his *first* wife. She had tried in vain to rule her first husband, but when she married her second, she took the reins into her own hands, and he submitted entirely to her government. As soon as the Milford estate came into her possession, she announced her dissatisfaction with the management of it, and resolved to change everything.

7*

It was in vain that her agent told her, that the building up of a town on her land had increased its value fourfold; she disapproved of long leases and low rents, and would alter all that. So down she came to Milford, with her husband and children, governess and servants, and put up at the Nelson Hotel. She began by disputing the leases which were granted, some for three lives, others for ninety-nine years. The ground-rent had been made low in order to induce people to build. She could not comprehend the policy of this, so she summoned her tenants to her presence. The upper class went, expecting to be received as guests, and to be complimented on the benefit they had bestowed on the estate, by building good houses upon it. Great, therefore, was their disappointment and indignation when they were received on the same footing as the humblest householder there, and told that their leases should all be broken. They appealed to the honorable husband of her Ladyship, but he sanctioned all she did. Every inhabitant became her enemy, though the event proved that she could not put her threat into execution.

Not satisfied with this aggressive act, she next attacked the Royal Dock-Yard, which it had cost Charles Greville the greatest exertion of his interest with the government to have established there, and which, with the whale fishery, was the cause of the rapid growth of the town. A piece of rough, rocky land, of no value to Lady Mansfield, or to any one else, had been wrongfully enclosed within the boundary of the dock-yard, and she claimed it so vehemently, that a commissioner was sent down from London to look into the matter. He looked too deeply into the affair for the benefit of her Ladyship. He reported that the site was wholly unfit for a building-yard, and recommended the removal of the whole concern to the other side of the haven, and several miles higher up, where he had discovered a tract of land belonging to Government, and admirably adapted to the purpose. In due time orders came to take down the vessels, then on the stocks, and remove them to the new dock-yard, near Pembroke, with all the materials belonging to his Majesty.

My father was so tormented by Lady Mansfield, that he also removed his fishery from Milford, and the town was left without any business of consequence. A large house, built by my father, was burnt down as soon as completed, and as her ladyship had disputed his lease, she could not oblige him to rebuild it, so the ultimate loss was hers. She did, at last, so ruin the place, that she never dared to show her face there again, and it was said of Milford, that you might fire a cannon down the Main street, without danger of hitting any one.

Only twenty miles from Milford was the pleasant sea-side resort called Tenby, little known in my day, but now a fashionable bathing-place. It was a small town, of poor houses, built on a projecting point of land, with a fine hard sand-beach on each side, giving the bathers the choice of the north or south sands. Curiously shaped rocks form the coast, and one large cave, which is filled with water at high tide, but remains empty many hours in the day, was once the scene of great alarm to a governess and three little girls who were caught in it by the tide. She, who should have seen to the safety of her charge, was so absorbed by an agreeable book, that she did not observe the rising tide, till the possibility of retreat was cut off by it. She was terribly frightened, but concealed her alarm from the children, as well as she could, and made them climb up to a high ledge of rock and sit there with her. To pass away the time, she told them stories; but they grew very weary, and when the bottom of the cave was filled with water, and the waves began to dash upon the rocks beneath their feet, they were much terrified, and it was all the governess could do to comfort them and assuage their fears, whilst her own courage was ebbing fast; at last the youngest child fell asleep in her arms and the other two nestled close to her, on either side. There was no higher ledge of rock on which they could sit, and she feared they would fall into the flood below if she attempted to make them stand on the rock they were sitting on. As soon as the arched entrance into the cave was covered by the advancing tide, they were in perfect darkness, and that added much to the fearfulness of their position. At last the children cried out, in distressed tones, that their feet were wet and the water was coming all over them. To which the governess replied, "Mine have been wet for some time; but never mind that; I don't think it will come higher than our knees." It was only after some mental exercise and earnest prayer that she was able to say this. Her words proved true. The tide did rise to her lap, and swelled up against them and all around them fearfully; but in a few more minutes its force seemed less, and presently they could be certain that it began to lower. Relieved from their terror, the two older children fell asleep, and then the governess was very anxious lest they should fall from their narrow perch and be drowned after all. Very long did the time seem before the tide retreated far enough for a little light to enter at the top of the entrance to the cave; but at length that light came, and not long after was heard the welcome sound of voices, and as soon as a boat could enter, one came to their relief, with the father of the children in it.

He found his little girls refreshed by their nap, and as lively and full of prattle as if no trouble had come near them; but their unhappy governess was utterly overcome. She could do nothing but weep, and afterwards fell into melancholy and died insane.

Another instance of the dangers of the sea to those on land occurs to me. A lady of my acquaintance, living by the seaside in England, walked down to the beach, accompanied by her two little girls and their tutor, to see the surf after a storm. They passed round a high projecting cliff, which was then far enough from the water for them to walk round it dry-shod. The grandeur of the waves and the curious things the children found in the rock-pools, beguiled the time, and when, on their way back, they reached the cliff, they found that the surf had sent some of its waters to the foot of it. They thought they could easily pass round it, if they did not mind wetting their feet, so the mother gathered up her dress and told the little girls to follow her. Just as she was passing the cliff, a wave dashed up and bore her off into the sea, where she was drowned, and the children were only saved by the tutor's catching hold of them and pulling them back. They returned home by another and a longer way, to carry to their father the astounding news that their mother was drowned. He rushed down to the fatal spot, but saw no sign of what had happened; he haunted the shore by day and by night, and had men watching all the time, in hopes of recovering the body, but it never appeared.

Another and a very different kind of danger attending a residence by the sea, was told by a descendant of the family in which it occurred, at a breakfast to which I was invited.

In a very large, old-fashioned habitation, perched on the brow of a beetling cliff, on the South coast of England, lived a widowed lady and her children, with a large retinue of servants, and every luxury that wealth could give, but without the society of neighbors. The nearest town was several miles off, and there were no country-seats near them; but the estate had been long in the family, and, though rather lonely, it was a favorite residence. The house had originally been a castle; but had been so altered and added to that little remained of its former appearance. Various rooms indicated, by their furniture and the pictures on the walls, the time to which they belonged; and long corridors led to many apartments never used by the family. It did, however, happen that a person was ill in one of these distant rooms, and a nurse, who was watching the sick woman, was greatly terrified by seeing the head of one of the old portraits on the wall move like a living one. She was sure that the eyes winked, and the head moved up and down. She was transfixed with terror, but controlled herself so far as not to scream. When she recovered the power of moving, she ran off to tell her mistress what she had seen, and that she could not possibly return to that haunted chamber. Several persons went to the room, but saw no motion in the old picture, and the poor nurse was well laughed at for her alarm. The next night, the housekeeper offered to watch in that same chamber, and she was sent screaming through the corridor by the same motion in the picture. The sick person was now removed to another part of the house, and the haunted chamber was locked up and never used.

Some time after this occurrence, the oldest son returned from a long absence in the army, and on hearing of the haunted chamber, he declared that he would find out if there were any marvellous appearances, by passing a night there himself. His mother and sisters tried in vain to dissuade him from it: the young soldier chose to show that he had no fear of ghosts or burglars. He said he should not go to bed; he would sit up armed, and have a bright wood fire or a good lamp to read by.

The family retired, leaving him to what they considered a useless vigil; but the next morning he joined them, looking very pale and haggard, and refused to say whether anything had occurred or not. He locked up the room, and forbade any one going near it. In a few days he told his mother that they must all quit that house, and live elsewhere. She asked him if he were going to bring a wife there, as the estate was his. He said no; that he should pull down the house, and raze it to the ground. "That is a new way to get rid of ghosts," said his mother. "This is to get rid of what is worse than ghosts," was his reply. But he refused all further explanation.

The old mansion was pulled down, and many years after it became known that a cave, under that wing of the castle which contained the haunted room, was used by smugglers, who wished to frighten the family from occupying the rooms above that cave, lest they should hear the noises they made in carrying their brandy casks into it. One of the gang had cut a hole through a thin partition between the chamber and a dressing-room, and made the aperture just behind a large portrait. He had removed the painting from the frame, and put himself in its place, on purpose to frighten the family, and make them think the chamber was haunted. This plan succeeded so well that the smugglers would have kept that part of the castle uninhabited, had it not been for the conduct of the son and heir of the house. When he was watching there, and occupied with his book, two smugglers entered suddenly through a trap-door in the dressing-room, and presenting their pistols to his breast, ordered him to remove from the table where his arms were laid. A third and fourth man entered and disposed of them. They then told him that they were smugglers, and used a cave underneath, and swore they would carry him off and kill him, unless he took an oath never to speak of what happened that night, and to pull down the whole house.

CHAPTER XX.

MARIAGES DE CONVENANCE.

IN Paris, where every father thinks he has an undoubted right to dispose of his children in marriage, according to his own ideas of expediency, I heard the most vehement denunciation of the practice, in a public lecture by Professor Chasles of the Institute, a little dark man, with a monkey face and gestures to match. He took for his subject Dickens's story of "Hard Times," in which a delicate young girl, educated at home, and entirely ignorant of the world, is made, by her father, to marry one of his business friends, who is twice her age, and very vulgar and disagreeable besides. She bears her trials with stoical endurance, putting a constant restraint upon her words and actions, and locking up within her own breast all the bitter feelings to which her situation gives rise.

At last she makes the acquaintance of a man whom she *could* love, and then she feels the full force of her wretched connection with a man whom she cannot love. Her good principles prevent her from giving way to this new-born passion; but she can no longer live with her husband, and, in her extremity of suffering, she resolves to tell her father the whole truth, and call on him to save her from sin and misery, by separating her from her uncongenial partner. That interview, between the father and daughter, is one of thrilling interest; nothing can be more forcibly portrayed than the utter wretchedness of such a marriage, and the dangers to which it leads.

With this for his subject, the Professor was eloquent in his denunciation of *mariages de convenance*, and his audience sympathized with him. Any one hearing his vehemence, and the plaudits which followed, would have supposed that the time had fully come for such marriages to be done away with forever. But alas! they are still going on.

I knew a young girl who had the courage to resist one of these forced marriages; but she had English as well as French blood in her veins. She and her brother (we will call them Antoinette and Philippe) were the children of a French officer married to an English lady. He died when they were young, and, on their mother's marrying a second time, they were sent to the care of an uncle and aunt in Paris, who had no children, and who brought up their niece and nephew as well as if they had been their own. When Antoinette was old enough to leave school, her uncle began to look out for a suitable match for her, and no one seemed to him so desirable as a rich old bachelor who was his intimate friend, and an *habitué* of the house.

When the aunt informed her niece that a husband was found for her, she was much surprised; but when told who it was, she could not believe that her aunt was in earnest; so she treated it as a joke, and laughed at the idea of her ever marrying that old gentleman, on whose knee she had sat from childhood up. When compelled, at last, to believe that her aunt was in earnest, she protested against the match, and declared it should never take place. Her aunt said nothing then, but began to make the necessary preparations, and always spoke as if it were a settled affair, and called the gentlemen her *futur*.

The unhappy girl felt as if chains were silently forming around her, and all her efforts to break loose from them were fruitless. She consulted her brother, who was a little older than herself. He advised her to talk with her uncle. She dared not do it, unless he would accompany her; but he very wisely refused, saying, "I had better not appear in the matter till you have tried all your means of escape, and, when you fail, I will come to your aid. You shall never marry that man." Encouraged by this, she ventured to remonstrate with her uncle; but he treated her opposition with supreme contempt, and told her his decision was irrevocable, and she would live to thank him for it. He said young girls knew nothing about married life, and must always abide by the judgment of their friends. Driven to despair by this talk with her uncle, she sought her brother, and told him she would drown herself in the Seine rather than submit to this hated marriage. He calmed her fears, advised her to behave as if she were resigned to her fate, and he would run off with her to England as soon as he could make the necessary preparations. He arranged everything so well, that he did carry off his sister, and place her in safety with her mother; but, in so doing, he felt that he was ruining his own prospects in life. His uncle would be so enraged at what he had done, as never to receive him again. His step-father was a wise and good man. He undertook to make his peace with his uncle, and, after a long correspondence, Philippe was allowed to return to his studies in Paris, and became eventually his uncle's heir. Antoinette remained under the roof of her step-father, who kept a boarding-school for boys. One of these fell in love with the handsome French girl. As he was an only son, and heir to a large fortune, her mother, from a sense of honor, did all she could to prevent the growth of this love affair. But the young folks kept it up, and became mutually attached.

Having run away once to avoid a match, it was very natural that Antoinette should think now of running away to secure a union with the youth she loved. So off they went one fine morning, and were lost to pursuit in a large city, where they remained hidden for two weeks, and then they suddenly appeared at our house in Bath. As they entered, I was reading a letter from Antoinette's mother, asking me if I knew where her daughter was, and imploring me to tell her if I did. The bridegroom was such a darling of his widowed mother that he could not offend her; and when she saw his bride, she was so fascinated by her that she welcomed her as a daughter; and this love match proved a very happy one. I say this one did, for I would not be supposed to mean that all love matches are happy, or that all interested matches are unhappy; but I do consider that all marriages, not founded on a strong and disinterested attachment, are wrong, and entail untold misery on the wretched beings so yoked.

In connection with this subject, I remember talking about it to a large class of young girls assembled in the studio of a female artist in Paris, to learn crayon drawing. My younger sister went there to take lessons, and I went with her. We were introduced as "*les demoiselles Anglaises.*" As soon as the teacher had placed my sister's easel, and given her a subject to copy, she left the room; and no sooner was she gone than all drawing ceased, and one young lady asked me if, in England, we did not marry for love. I told her we did, and then they were all very anxious to know how that could be brought about. "*Comment cela se fait il,*" resounded from all sides. Feeling very willing to stir up a mutinous spirit against *mariages de convenance,* I gave them a full description of the intercourse allowed in England between young girls and young men of the same class. I spoke of country life there, with its fine large mansions filled with guests, whose amusements were riding, walking, boating, fishing, balls, and parties. I told them how preferences were shown, and how returned, and described all the steps that led to a love match, approved, though not made, by the parents. Those poor young creatures listened to me as if their lives depended on what I was saying; and when I had done, a general exclamation of wonder and admiration made so much noise that I could only hear distinctly what a girl near me said. "English wives are held up to us as models of virtue; but I do not see what merit they have when they *choose* their husbands. It is easy enough to be a good wife to a man of your choice."

Here the teacher entered, scolded the girls for having done so little, and the lesson ended. On our way home, my sister found fault with my having given such a favorable picture of love-matches in England, and said she should, at the next lesson, tell them how many of those love-matches proved, in time, to be very unhappy ones. She thought it was unkind to make them earnestly desire what they could not possibly obtain.

I have known women in England who had too much sentiment to marry for money, or for an establishment, or indeed from any selfish motive, but who were willing to sacrifice themselves for the sake of some advantage to be gained by a beloved brother, or sister, or mother,—not being at all aware that in so doing they were committing a sin. Several instances of this mistaken generosity have come under my observation, and it has always resulted in the sacrifice being made in vain, for the person who was to be benefited died, and the poor victim lived a long life of wretchedness.

I was well acquainted with one of those unhappy wives. She and her brother were left orphans when very young, and had been brought up by an uncle, a sordid and hard-hearted man. Having no affection lavished upon them by ——, they were all the more attached to each other. When the boy grew up, his uncle intended to place him in some situation wholly distasteful to him, while there was another career open to him which he much desired. I forget what either of them was, but I know that the uncle agreed to let his nephew follow his inclination, on one condition only, and that was that his sister should marry a rich linen draper, whose suit she had rejected, and for whom she felt a great distaste. She belonged to a class much above a retail shopkeeper in London, and felt it a degradation to be married to one. After a long and painful struggle, her love for her brother triumphed over all other feelings, and when he had obtained the situation he desired, she gave her hand to the linen draper, who had behaved very well during his courtship. Immediately after the marriage ceremony, the bride and groom set off on a wedding tour. On stopping to dine at a hotel, they ordered a roast fowl for their dinner. When it was served the bridegroom cut off both wings, with the meat of the breast, for himself, and pushed the remains over to his bride. She thought at first that he was doing it as a good joke, and expected her share of the white meat; but he was far enough from joking. He was beginning that course of conduct which he continued all through life, as a retaliation for her refusal of his first offer, and as the means of taking down her pride, and showing her that he was her lord and master. Her condition was one of hopeless misery; her brother's happiness was her only consolation, and that was taken from her by his early death.

CHAPTER XXI.

UNHAPPY MARRIAGES.

ANOTHER instance occurs to me of the wretchedness consequent upon marriages without love, in the case of a very young girl sacrificed to the sordid calculations of a weak and ambitious mother. Too young to comprehend what she was about, she was led as a lamb to the slaughter.

A worldly-minded mother, with seven grown-up daughters, must, in England, have her head full of schemes, and her heart full of anxiety, as to how to dispose of them in marriage. Men in that country are more careful than in this, how they enter into matrimony before they have ample means to support a wife, and those who have sufficient incomes are slower in making a choice. Mrs. B—— was therefore much pleased when a wealthy merchant proposed for her fourth daughter; but he was not fully accepted when her youngest girl, Olivia, came home from school for the last time, and was to begin her career as a young lady. She was the prettiest one of the family, and the greatest favorite of her mother, who felt a pang of jealousy for her, that any of her sisters should be married before her.

Mrs. B—— remembered that the gentleman now paying his addresses to her daughter, had a brother older than himself, who was also a bachelor, and she determined to do all in her power to secure him for her darling child. Disparity of years was of no consequence in her view, compared with the fact that, as the oldest son he had inherited the largest portion of a wealthy father's property, and she thought with much satisfaction that, as his wife, Olivia would take precedence of her elder sister. Mrs. B—— gave the younger brother to understand that if he wished his own suit to prosper, he must find a match for Olivia. On this he proposed to his brother to pay his addresses to that pretty girl, and he readily consented, for he had always followed in the footsteps of his father, and as he married at forty years of age, the son would do the same. So Mrs. B—— had the satisfaction of marrying two daughters on the same day, and seeing the younger one take precedence of her elder sister. So much for the feelings of the mother; but what were those of the favorite child, who was thus disposed of? As she was in after life an intimate friend of mine, I have heard from her own lips, all the circumstances of her union with that rich old bachelor, who never knew an emotion of love, was perfectly indifferent to her when he married her, and continued so throughout his life. She told me that as soon as she left her boarding-school, she began to read romances, and was so absorbed by them that she took little notice of what was passing around her, until her mother told her she had a suitor, and would probably be married as soon as her sister. When introduced to her future husband she thought him very unlike the lovers she had been reading about, but her mother told her that real husbands were always very different from the heroes of romance. She thought she ought to be in love with Mr. N—— before she married him, but was told that that would come afterwards; and so, knowing nothing of life, a mere child of seventeen, and young of her years, she was hurried into the bonds of matrimony, and most irksome did she find them!

As the wife of the oldest son, she was made mistress of a sombre old mansion, in the midst of the busiest part of the city of London, and had for her companions two very stiff and formal maiden sisters of her husband. A sad change this from her father's cheerful villa a few miles from London, and the large family party she had left. She complained of having nothing to do, and her sisters-in-law immediately bought a piece of linen, cut it up into shirts for their brother, and told her that making them would be a pleasant occupation for her, and a proper thing for a wife to do. She has laughed since at the docility with which she set to work on those shirts, stitching away all the morning, from after breakfast till luncheon time, at one. At two she and the two old ladies took an airing in her new coach, and returned the few visits she received from her husband's city friends. After a six o'clock dinner, she was expected to play whist all the evening till bedtime.

This dreadfully dull life went on through the winter and spring; but when summer came, Mr. N—— remembered that his honored parents always spent a few weeks every year at some watering-place; so he would take his wife and sisters to Weymouth.

There, for the first time, this pretty young wife saw something of the gay world. She was in a large hotel, full of company, and dined every day at the public table. Her youth and beauty and simple manners attracted much admiration and attention, and she began to feel that she was of some importance in that society. A new life opened before her; she became a general favorite with persons of refinement and of fashion, such as she had never known before. This social sunshine developed in her new powers of observation and reflection, and gave her courage to express her thoughts and feelings as she had never before done.

Every one invited her to ride, or walk, or drive with them; and instead of playing whist with her husband every evening, she was dancing and playing round games with the gayest young people. Mr. N—— and his sisters found plenty of elderly persons ready to play whist with them, and were so well amused that they cared not what Olivia was doing. They little thought that she was imbibing ideas and feelings and tastes which would make the monotony of her home intolerable, would change her whole character, and revolutionize her life.

It was not long before some of her fashionable admirers began to hint at her being a neglected wife, and to wonder how it was possible for one so young and so charming to be treated with so much indifference. This shocked her, as an indelicate observation for any one to make to a wife, and she resented it accordingly; but it opened her eyes to a painful truth of which she had hardly been conscious before, but which now became more apparent to her every day.

The striking contrast between her husband's behavior to her, both before and after marriage, and that lover-like attention she was now receiving from the most elegant and fascinating men in the hotel, convinced her that she had made a fatal mistake in marrying Mr. N——, and that there were men in the world who resembled the heroes of romance of whom she used to read.

There was one man of high birth, elegant manners, and great personal beauty, who exerted all his powers of fascination to make the neglected wife in love with him; but she was proof against all his seductions. French novels had not then corrupted the young mind, nor was the dangerous doctrine of affinities then known. She had strict notions of a wife's duty to her husband, and acted accordingly. She even forced herself to tell Mr. N—— that Captain C—— made love to her, and she thought they had better go home. Instead of valuing this confidence, and strengthening her virtue by a grateful approval, he only said, "Pooh, pooh! child; don't fancy that every man who pays you a compliment is in love with you. I shall not go home till our six weeks are expired."

Chagrined and provoked at her husband's way of receiving what it had cost her such a severe struggle to say, she felt inclined to listen with more indulgence to the sentimental conversation of the gallant Captain. She would not allow him to make protestations of love, but she received with pleasure the flattering attentions paid her by him and several other gentlemen, making no distinction between them, and doing her best to conceal from Captain C—— the preference she felt for him. Delivered from this great danger by her conscientiousness and her native delicacy, she was still bent on securing the acquaintance of the most agreeable of her fellow-boarders, and when she returned to London, she received their calls, and, from that time, she had a very different set of visitors from those to whom her husband had introduced her. Her maiden sisters-in-law soon found that she had escaped from their tutelage; and not enjoying her new friends, they made long visits to their other brothers. Thus left to her own desires, she filled her spare beds with new guests, and had frequent small dinner-parties, to the surprise of her husband, who always went to his counting-room at nine in the morning, and never returned until time to dress for a six o'clock dinner. He would remonstrate with her on having so much company, but did not absolutely forbid it.

When the London season came round, she thought it necessary to her success with her fashionable friends to give a ball. She knew her husband would never consent to it, so she called it a *party*, and kept him entirely in the dark about it until the evening arrived, when his astonishment made him dumb, and the presence of so many fine people imposed upon him the necessity of treating them civilly.

They had excellent music and a luxurious supper, provided and put on table by the celebrated Gunter.

The fashionables from the West End of London were surprised to find that the wife of a merchant, living in the city, could give such an elegant ball, and the novelty made it very agreeable to them.

Never having been truly united to her husband, her new mode of living made the separation wider than ever, and she seemed to regard him only as the paymaster of her establishment, and the provider of good wines for her guests. He was a lover of routine, and when his wife's frequent dinner-parties and annual ball recurred every year, he made no further opposition to them. He did, however, become tired of going to fashionable watering-places, and she agreed to give them up, if he would have a house in the country and live there half the year. He accordingly bought a very nice place, within five miles of London, near to her father's residence, and not far from the homes of his two married brothers. It suited him much better than it did her, to be thus planted in the midst of their relations. He was very fond of them all, but her tastes and feelings separated her from them, and I have heard her describe the family dinners that she was obliged to partake of once a week, as a real martyrdom to her. Her avowed dislike to these reunions gave great offence, and many bitter and sarcastic speeches were made about her preference of new and fashionable friends, to old and tried ones.

Mrs. N—— was a member of the Episcopal Church and a constant attendant upon its services, and she would have been greatly shocked had any one told her that she was without religion; but certainly the blessed influence of the Holy Spirit, promised us by our Divine Master, had not yet purified and elevated her mind. She was still of the earth, earthy, and her conduct at this time was that of a foolish woman of the world. She brought a hornet's nest about her ears, and suffered much from its stings.

The next change, for the better, in her mode of life, was brought about by the introduction into this formal family-circle of a middle-aged bachelor, distinguished for his scientific attainments, his learning, and his artistic tastes. Alarmed by the pointed attentions paid him by the single ladies in this circle, he naturally took refuge with a pretty married woman, whose tastes were more like his own, whose house was always open to him, to whose pleasant dinners he was always invited, and whose carriage was ever at his service.

He was a wise and good man, and saw at once that wedlock had brought no happiness to his agreeable hostess, and that she was suffering from want of interesting occupation; so he endeavored to interest her in the study of botany, and found her a very apt scholar. They walked together in search of specimens, and he taught her how to examine and classify them, and so great was her industry and perseverance that she soon had an herbarium which contained all the plants in that neighborhood. Her friend next turned her attention to mineralogy, in which he had an extensive and valuable collection. She bought a cabinet, and he gave her his duplicate specimens to begin with, and introduced her to the auction-room, where she could increase her collection. He induced her to study enough of geology and chemistry to understand the nature and value of the minerals she bought, and this pursuit gave her great pleasure. None of her relations could comprehend this. They thought that she only pretended to like her new occupation, in order to engross the attention of her learned friend, and they were very jealous of her.

To associate, for the first time, with a highly cultivated and scientific man, to be the only one in a large circle capable of entering into his pursuits, and to be the chief object of his attentions, might well excite her gratitude and esteem, and she naturally wished to return some of his favors, by putting her house, her carriage, and her time at his disposal.

A mineralogist always has unsatisfied desires for some rare specimen, and Mrs. N—— would spend days in a dirty auction-room, waiting to secure for her friend some stone that she knew he wished to possess, and long evenings were spent in talking over the treasures they had collected.

Things had gone on for two years in the same way, when Mrs. N—— invited to her house a young girl, who added to a good education a general culture, a taste for the fine arts, and a love for science. She was a very agreeable addition to Mrs. N—— and her friend,—more especially the latter,—who was becoming rather tired of his perpetual *tête à tête* with his pupil, and was well pleased to come in contact with a fresh and vigorous mind, already well cultivated, and fond of some of his favorite pursuits. This guest was from the country, and she must be shown the sights of London. The scientific man condescended to be her showman, and most ably did he perform his part. He obtained tickets of admission to all the finest private collections of pictures, and gave his companions the benefit of his knowledge of the various merits of the ancient masters. Whatever sight was to be seen, he made it doubly interesting by his learning and his taste. All the best theatres were visited in turn, and there Mr. N—— accompanied them, making himself the escort of the young lady, and leaving his wife to "her philosopher," as he used to call him.

At the end of a few weeks, this trio was broken up, and the *tête à tête* was resumed for another year, being carried on as well during the six months in the city, as in the country.

By this time, the "envy, malice, and all uncharitableness" of the family circle had reached a fearful height, and led to the aspersion of Mrs. N——'s character. They accused her and her friend of too great an intimacy, and even spread the slander among their acquaintances, and endeavored thereby to deprive Mrs. N—— of a second visit from her congenial young friend. She was however so thoroughly convinced of the falsehood of the charge, that she treated it with silent contempt, and paid the expected visit. The result of her careful examination of the parties was, that perfect delicacy and propriety marked their intercourse, that no tender sentiment existed on his side, but that on hers she was struggling to conceal a love that amounted to idolatry. This generous young friend determined to do all she could to save the reputation and future well-being of Mrs. N——, even at the expense of some present happiness. She sought a private interview with the philosopher, told him of the slanders which were in circulation, and besought him not to compromise the reputation of his friend by continuing his great intimacy. He replied, "You are a brave woman, to dare to speak so to me, and I honor you for it. I have wished a thousand times to break my chains, but I am so bound by innumerable obligations to the lady, that it seems like the blackest ingratitude to break up the intimacy." — "Your obligations to her should make you careful of her good repute; better be thought ungrateful than be the cause of a real injury." — "You are right; I see it all now, as I never did before; I will cut the connection at once." — "Do not be too rash; break off by degrees; you are going to Scotland for several months, do not write to her during your absence, and when you return, visit her only as a common acquaintance. This advice was followed, the lady's reputation was saved, and though she suffered for a while, she realized the danger she had escaped, and sought occupation and interest in establishing a boarding-school for twelve poor orphans, whom she fed and clothed and educated out of her own allowance for *pin-money*.

She survived her husband many years, and became a great traveller; but whether she ever found her way into the "kingdom of God on earth," I do not know, for I lost sight of her when I came to this country.

CHAPTER XXII.

GREENWICH OBSERVATORY. — MRS. SOMERVILLE. — DR. ROBINSON. — OBSERVATORY AT ARMAGH.

WHEN travelling in Europe, it is a great advantage to belong to some profession, or to be devoted to some special object, as that introduces you to persons of similar pursuits, who feel a pleasure in forwarding your views, and pay you attentions accordingly.

I never was aware of this until I travelled with my husband, who was an astronomer and mathematician, and so well known as such, in England, that the Professor of Mathematics in Cambridge wrote to him, "Come to Cambridge; you need bring no letters of introduction; we all know you, and we want to see you."

When Mr. Farrar visited the Royal Observatory at Greenwich, I was allowed to accompany him, and the gentleman who received us, told me that I was enjoying a privilege which no duchess in the land could command. So much for being the wife of an astronomer.

No spot in England was visited by the Harvard Professor with so much interest as that plain one-story building, on a small but abrupt hill, in Greenwich Park. We went all over it just before noon, and wished to see the observer take the sun's meridian, but that was not allowed, for it was a matter of such nice observation, that the mere breathing of another person in the room might spoil its accuracy. This fact interested him. He looked with reverence on a spot which had been the fountain of such rich streams of science, and was so intimately connected with the history of astronomy.

As soon as that distinguished astronomer, Mrs. Somerville, heard that Mr. Farrar was in London, she sent him a message by Lucy Aiken, to ask him to come and see her, and to say she would be at home every morning during the next week, till he came, that she might be sure to see him. She sent me word that she never made any calls, or she would come to see me, but she hoped I would accompany my husband.

We of course obeyed this gratifying summons, and went down to Chelsea early in the week. Dr. Somerville was governor of the hospital there for invalid soldiers, and lived in the building, where he had a handsome suite of apartments. He met us in the hall, and ushered us into a large room, which seemed to be a library and drawing-room all in one. There sat the pretty, refined, and elegant woman, who had astonished the scientific world by her translation and thorough comprehension of La Place's grand work on the mechanism of the heavens. She received us most cordially, and after a few minutes of general conversation, Dr. Somerville invited me to the other end of the room to look at a cabinet of minerals, collected by his wife. While showing them, he was continually looking over his shoulder at Mrs. Somerville and Mr. Farrar. At last he exclaimed, "Ah! they have got at it now; I thought they would, if we left them alone." Sure enough, they were talking away on the higher branches of mathematics and astronomy.

Several oil paintings, of Swiss scenery, attracted my observation, and Dr. Somerville told me they were done by his wife, from sketches made from nature, and that her favorite recreation was a tour in Switzerland. He showed me also a collection of botanical specimens gathered there. So I discovered that this great mathematician was also a botanist, mineralogist, and artist.

The two astronomers so enjoyed talking together, that I was obliged, at last, to interrupt them and remind my husband that it was time to go. Mrs. Somerville would not let us depart without naming a day when we would dine with her, and meet the Astronomer Royal, Mr. Bailey. That done, we drove back to town, delighted with our visit. Mr. Farrar was full of admiration for the extraordinary attainments of Mrs. Somerville, and not less charmed by her feminine graces and modest unpretending manners.

Our dinner visit proved equally agreeable. We then saw her two grown-up daughters, and met the Astronomer Royal. The conversation was on common topics; the dinner was simple — not many dishes — but everything of the best; and I observed that the footman took his orders about the dinner from his master. As the Doctor was obliged to cater for the hospital, I suppose he took the care of providing for his own table. Mrs. Somerville's exquisite toilette and the dressing of her beautiful brown hair showed that the most abstruse studies had detracted nothing from a proper womanly attention to appearances.

When the ladies retired from the dinner-table, we all looked over a box of birds just arrived from South America, and admired their brilliant plumage. They were prepared for stuffing, with the flesh and bones taken out, and the box contained a great number of them. Leaving the young ladies to talk ornithology over them, I asked Mrs. Somerville to tell me what first turned her attention to mathematics, and she very readily gave me the following particulars.

Her father, Admiral Fairfax, was constantly at

sea, in the service of his country, and her mother lived in a very retired spot in Scotland, during his absence. The only village near them was within walking distance, and the family often went there to make small purchases, and visit the rooms of the dressmaker and milliner, who took a magazine which contained the fashions. Looking over it one day, Mrs. Somerville saw some questions given which were to be answered by algebra. She did not know what algebra was, but she thought she could answer them by an arithmetical calculation. This she did very easily, and in the next number of the magazine she saw that she was right. Her curiosity, however, was excited as to what algebra was, and she made inquiries of Dr. Somerville, the father of her present husband. He referred her to the article on algebra in the Encyclopædia, which he possessed, and she carried the heavy volume home. She soon understood the subject, and was delighted with that method of doing sums. Her father was with them in Edinburgh the following winter, and there she found the aid she needed, and pursued her studies into the higher branches of mathematics, and became so fond of the science, that it has since been her most delightful occupation.

When we ordered our carriage to return to town Dr. Somerville asked if we could give Mr.

Bailey a seat in it, which we were happy to do. The two astronomers talked incessantly all the way to London, and I listened in silent amazement, at not being able to understand anything they said. They seemed to me to be talking in hints and half-spoken phrases; they were so familiar with their subject that a word or two was sufficient to convey their ideas; but to me they were unintelligible. The effect was very curious of having people converse in English, without being able to comprehend what they said.

I was told, by a common friend, that Mrs. Somerville was a good Greek and Latin scholar, and that she spoke French and Italian well; but she told me herself that she never could learn German, and she had tried hard; for it was the favorite language of her daughters, who always spoke it to each other.

I saw Mrs. Somerville but once more, and then she did me the favor of calling on me in London, and spending an hour. She was then full of feeling for a friend in affliction, and talked chiefly of her. Mrs. Somerville was married twice, and this gave rise to the mistake which made La Place say, that he was astonished to hear that there were two Englishwomen who could understand his *Mécanique Céleste.* After her second marriage she was in Paris, and La Place called to see her. He found a lady in her saloon, with whom he talked for some time of the opera and the *on dits* of the day. After a while, he said, he had called to see Madame Somerville, and hoped she was at home, when to his surprise, he found that the pretty woman he was talking with was the lady herself.

We made the acquaintance of another very agreeable astronomer, Dr. Robinson of the Observatory at Armagh, to whom Miss Edgeworth gave us a letter of introduction, and of whom she spoke in such high terms that we altered our route on purpose to see him.

We arrived at the inn at Armagh on a Saturday morning, and despatched our letter to the Doctor. He sent word that he would call in the morning, and the next day he was with us before church time, invited us to sit in his pew, to dine with his family at five o'clock, and to look at his instruments in the evening. In this first interview we were willing to believe that all Miss Edgeworth had said of him was true. I thought him one of the most agreeable men I had ever met with.

We attended cathedral service in a small chapel of ease, which was used while the cathedral was being restored, and, after the service, Dr. Robinson took us all over the ancient edifice, and talked of it with the science of an architect and the enthusiasm of an antiquary, showing us how the best things in it had been covered up by centuries of patching. At that time the Bishop of Armagh was Lord John Beresford, a single man with a large fortune besides his church benefice, the emoluments of which he devoted to public works. He had given eight thousand pounds to the repairs of the cathedral.

Dr. Robinson took us to the top of the cathedral tower, whence we had a fine view of the town and the adjacent country. We saw the Primate's house and park, the monument erected to employ the poor, the court-house, library, and other public buildings. While conversing about the soil and population of Ireland, Dr. Robinson told us there were four hundred inhabitants to every square mile, and said, "With this fertile soil and abundant power of labor, this land might be one of the most prosperous in the world, were it not for bad legislation and Papacy." After much pleasant chat, Dr. Robinson left us. A little before five o'clock we walked up to the Observatory, where, in a neat stone house attached to it, the astronomer lived. We were most cordially received by Mrs. Robinson, and partook of a nice family dinner with two other guests and two young sons of the Doctor. After dinner we were shown into the Observatory, and Mr. Farrar was much interested in seeing some of Dr. Robinson's improvements and contrivances for rendering his means of observation the most perfect in the world. The American astronomer had labored for years for the establishment of an observatory in Cambridge, Mass., and had not relinquished the hope, so he looked with peculiar interest at the arrangements of the Observatory in Armagh. We were both so absorbed in the subject, that Mrs. Robinson could hardly get us into the house again when tea was ready.

A cloudy night prevented our seeing the heavenly bodies, but our host amused us with a very fine microscope, which was equally good by lamp or sunlight. The subjects were well selected and beautifully arranged, and Dr. Robinson held forth upon them as though his peculiar vocation had been natural history instead of astronomy. Among numerous other curiosities, we were shown the difference of structure between the fibre of cotton and flax, — a difference which has settled the question of whether cotton was known to the ancient Egyptians, and proved all the mummy cloth to be linen. Dr. Robinson talked of the new discoveries of the polarization of light in a way highly gratifying to Mr. Farrar, who had paid much attention to the subject. He put a thin piece of tourmaline into the microscope, making the light pass through it, and showing how certain colors were retained while others disappeared, — strained out, as it were. He showed us steel buttons, in which prismatic colors were produced by lines cut on them, so fine as to be invisible to the naked eye. Many other interesting objects were presented to us in this fine microscope, and the evening passed but too quickly away.

Mrs. Robinson appeared to be the worthy and congenial partner of the Doctor. A frank cordiality made us at once feel at ease as her guests. Taking care not to interfere with her husband's exhibitions, she, too, showed us many pretty things. Among them I remember a beautiful little temple, about eighteen inches high, with an equestrian statue on the top, and several full-length figures standing in it, all made by a young lady, in white card-paper. The cornices, volutes, carved friezes, and ceilings, were all done by cuttings in card-paper. It was of unsullied whiteness, much as it must have been handled in the making. We were told that the lady never worked on it in a room with a fire, for fear of its getting sullied. It was kept under a glass shade. We saw a paper clock, too, done in the same way.

It was late before we could put an end to this delightful visit, and on returning to our inn, it was long before we could subside into rest. The next morning we went again to the Observatory, by invitation of Dr. Robinson, who wished to show the American Professor more of his fine instruments and his peculiar contrivances for working with them to the best advantage. I remember only one of these, which was screwing on to his telescope, when not in use, a bottle of lime, to keep the speculum dry.

CHAPTER XXIII.

A REMARKABLE WOMAN.

THERE comes before me now, with great distinctness, the image of a very handsome and highly gifted woman, whose career was rather remarkable. She was about twenty-five years old when I became acquainted with her. We were both guests of an English gentleman, about to emigrate to America with a large family of motherless children, between the ages of ten and twenty. She came highly recommended, by an intimate friend of the family, to try whether she could make herself acceptable as a companion to the elder girls, and useful as a teacher to the younger ones. I was there to pass a few weeks with my oldest and dearest friends, before losing them forever in the backwoods of America, and I was to help the father, Mr. K——, to decide whether Miss D—— was the right person to accompany his children to the New World.

She immediately perceived that it was important for her to conciliate my good opinion, and she laid herself out to do it most successfully. I was charmed by her beauty, and by her varied powers and accomplishments. She had a rich and mellow voice, and sang by ear, without any accompaniment, and with more expression and feeling than any one I ever heard, except Jenny Lind. Her recitations, too, were wonderfully fine. She would stand up in the middle of the room and personate two or three characters in a play, and so change her voice that, with your eyes shut, you would suppose there were several speakers. She read aloud delightfully, and her narrating was equally excellent. With all these accomplishments she had not neglected the useful arts. She was a capital seamstress, and despatched her work with a rapidity that seemed like magic. If all women could sew as she did, sewing-machines need never to have been invented. The art of cooking was not less familiar to her. She had kept house for several years for a bachelor brother, in London, and was quite at home in all the details of housekeeping. She proved so delightful an addition to this family party in their quiet country life, that all were desirous that she should accompany them to America. We found out by degrees, that her relations were not aware of her being at Mr. K——'s, and knew nothing of her intention to expatriate herself; so he very properly told her he could not take her with him without the consent of her mother, who was her only surviving parent. This gave her great uneasiness, but after much hesitation, she consented to his having a personal interview with her mother, and asking her consent.

Mr. K—— was no sooner gone, than Miss D—— became very ill with a high fever, attended by spasms and delirium. As I was the oldest person in the house, and much interested in her, I became her nurse, and had the whole charge of her night and day. We had to send four miles for a physician, and he could only see her once in twenty-four hours. A great responsibility, therefore fell on me. Her delirium intermitted, and when she found she had been so affected, she seemed much alarmed, and begged me to tell her everything she had said, and not to let any one but myself be in the room when she was again delirious. I promised her I would not, and told her she had disclosed no secrets; that she fancied herself travelling in America, but not with the K—— family; they were always in advance of her, and she was trying to get up with them. She questioned me closely as to all she had said, and seemed satisfied at last that her secrets were safe. Sometimes, when delirious, she would sing most sweetly, in such subdued tones that it sounded as if it were afar off; and in the dead of night, when watching alone with her, these strains came like heavenly music, and I often thought they would usher her into the land of spirits. She had spasms of the muscles so violent, that when lying in bed, too weak to make any voluntary movement, she would rise directly up and throw herself on to the floor, at the foot of her bed. At last these spasms attacked her heart, and one night the physician remained with us, and with his finger on her pulseless wrist, expected every hour to be her last. That was the crisis of her disease. A warm bath relieved her, and she began to recover from that time. When Mr. K—— returned, having obtained the consent of her mother to her going to America, that news was to her as the elixir of life, and she recovered rapidly.

She had judged wisely in preferring a personal interview with her mother to any letter that Mr. K—— could have written, for there was that in his looks and manner which inspired confidence in all who conversed with him, and he had promised that anxious mother to be a father to her child, and that, if she continued with him to his death, she should have a daughter's portion of his property.

Preparations for quitting England were carried on now with great spirit and cheerfulness. I could not help wondering at the willingness of the whole family to quit their ancestral halls, until a conversation with Mr. K—— explained it.

He considered England on the eve of revolution. It was at the time when the people were clamoring for a Parliamentary reform, and the riots at Manchester and other places, made many fear a general uprising. Mr. K—— was a reformer, and was intimate with the radical leaders. He knew that in case there was an insurrection, he could not help taking a prominent part in it. He was old, and wished to avoid a bloody revolution. He admired a republican form of government, and desired of all things to live and die under it, and to establish his children in the United States. He had imbued them with his principles, and they all looked eagerly forward to being citizens of a free Republic.

A family with whom Mr. K—— had long been intimate, and whom we will call by the name of Lawless, intended to follow him to America, and their eldest son was already there, exploring the Western States, and fixing on a locality where they could make a settlement. Soon after the K——s landed in New York, he joined them, and persuaded them that the prairies of Illinois would be their "promised land." Several young Englishmen had emigrated with Mr. K——, and a large cavalcade proceeded westward on horseback. There were no railroads then.

Though their journey was long and sometimes wearisome, they found much to interest them in the natural productions of the country, and the manners and customs of the people. It was soon obvious to all the party that Mr. Lawless was devoted to Miss D——, and that they were very much in love with each other. When this was pointed out to Mr. K——, he said it could not be, for Mr. Lawless had a wife in England. That good old man thought too well of both the parties to believe they could do wrong, and great was his dismay and grief when Mr. Lawless informed him that he intended to marry Miss D——, and remain in a certain town through which they had passed. Mr. K—— remonstrated in vain, and was told that a suit was instituted against the wife in England, which would certainly end in divorce, and he only anticipated his freedom in marrying now.

Here, then, was the explanation of Miss D——'s anxiety to come to the United States. She only made use of the K——s in order to join her lover, and this was the secret she was so afraid of divulging in her delirium.

The marriage ceremony was performed, and she settled in a Western city, where she soon made friends and became the most popular woman there. Her domestic virtues claimed their approbation, and her accomplishments charmed them. She never made invidious comparisons between the Old World and the New; she accepted willingly all the novelties and peculiarities of the society she was in, and was too happy to find fault with anything. At the end of several months, her husband was obliged to go to England on business, and during his absence she became a mother. Nothing could exceed the kind attentions she received on that occasion. One elderly lady, the wife of a distinguished citizen, acted the part of mother to her, and she was made much of by all her friends.

While basking in this sunshine of social happiness, and never dreaming of a change, a rumor reached the city that she was not the legal wife of Mr. Lawless. She was too marked a character not to be much discussed, and at first the rumor was discredited; but at last information was received which left no doubt of its being a case of bigamy, and by the time her husband returned she had lost all her popularity, was deserted by her friends, and was glad to fly with him to the West, and lead the life of a pioneer's wife.

CHAPTER XXIV.

PRINCESS CHARLOTTE.

A YOUNG Princess, who is heir to the British throne, becomes an object of great interest and curiosity to every little girl in the kingdom, especially to those who are nearly of her own age; and the Princess Charlotte, daughter of George IV., was rendered peculiarly interesting by the unhappy circumstances of her childhood. Separated from her mother, tyrannized over by her father, over-disciplined by her grandmother and aunts, she was an object of love and pity to the nation. Very different was her bringing up from that which her cousin Victoria received from her judicious mother, the Duchess of Kent. The Princess Charlotte was *bequeened* from her very birth, and never knew what it was to be free from the restraints of royalty, while the Princess Victoria was treated like any nobleman's child, and was kept in ignorance of her being heir presumptive to the throne until she was ten years old, when she discovered it by looking into an almanac.

When the Princess Charlotte was four years

old, she was allowed to play with a little girl of her own age, and they were both to partake of a supper of bread and milk. A silver bowl and a gold spoon were given to the royal child, whilst her little companion had a china bowl and a silver spoon. This so displeased the Princess, that she threw herself on the floor and kicked and screamed for a china bowl and a silver spoon.

In this way her royal state was always made an irksome bondage to her; and it is not to be wondered at that a high-spirited child should sometimes prove restive under such senseless restraints. The public always sympathized with her, and heard with pleasure of her rebellious acts.

One of these I well remember hearing of at the time, and being rebuked for admiring it. Queen Charlotte, grandmother to the Princess, took her to task for her want of dignity in her manner of getting into her carriage. She told her she should never forget that she was the future queen of England. She promised to do differently next time, and so she did. For, refusing to be handed in as usual, she desired the attendants to stand back, and running violently through the hall, she leaped into the carriage at one bound, and, laughing merrily, told those near her to let the Queen know how dignified she was.

Besides having ladies in waiting, and governesses and tutors of all sorts, she had the Bishop of London for her adviser and religious teacher. Finding how very passionate she was, he wrote a short prayer for her to repeat every time she felt her anger rising. So one day when he visited her, he was told of her having been in a great passion with the head-governess, and he said that he feared she had not repeated the prayer he gave her. She replied, "O, yes, I did. I should have struck her if I had not said your prayer."

As soon as she was old enough to know anything about the separation of her parents, and their detestation of each other, she espoused her mother's cause, and was consequently much disliked by her father. She was removed from her mother's house at the age of eight years, and only allowed to see her once a week; but as she grew older, and became acquainted with her mother's wrongs, she kept up a secret correspondence with her, in spite of her father's commands and the watchful eyes around her. He suspected that her household favored this intercourse, and he determined to put a stop to it. In a private interview, he informed his daughter that he should change her household, and remove her to Cranbourn Lodge, in Windsor Forest. He then dismissed her, and told her to send Lady —— to him.

Shocked and alarmed by these sudden changes, dreading to be sent to a secluded spot, twenty miles from London, and fearing she would never be allowed to see her mother again, she resolved to rush off at once to Connaught House, and have at least one interview with her, before she was banished to Windsor Forest. Instead of sending her governess to her father, she ran down a back stair-case into the street, without bonnet or shawl, found a hackney-coach, jumped into it, and told the coachman to drive to Connaught Place. Arrived there she found that her mother was at Black Heath. She told the coachman to drive down to Black Heath. He said it was not possible for his horses to go so far. She told him who she was, and that he must take her to her mother. He was sorry not to oblige her, but his old nags would drop down by the way, and then where would *her Ladyship* be. According to the account I heard at the time, she then drove to the house of the Prime Minister, and, alighting there, begged him to order his carriage and send her in it to Black Heath. This he dared not do. He told her that she must obey her father; that he, as Regent, had absolute power over the persons of all the royal family while under age. She wished to see her mother's legal adviser, Lord Brougham, and he was sent for. Meanwhile the Prime Minister had sent a messenger to the Regent, to tell him where his daughter was, and that she would soon return home. Several important personages gathered round her, and many hours were consumed in listening to her complaints and endeavoring to reconcile her to her inevitable fate.

This extraordinary flight of the Princess, and her so bravely putting aside all the restraints of royalty for the sake of a parting interview with her mother, so touched all hearts capable of appreciating her feelings and the force of her character, that she became the idol of the people.

Even the hackney-coach she had used, and the old man who had driven her, were made of great importance. Thousands of persons were desirous, for her sake, of riding in that carriage. This proof of her popularity was very displeasing to the Regent, and he gave orders to have the coach destroyed, the horses shot, and the coachman sent away from London.

When the Prince of Wales became possessed of regal power, as Regent, he abandoned all his old friends, the Whigs, and allied himself with Tories. His daughter, being at a dinner-party at Carlton House, heard her father speak contemptuously of the very men whom he had formerly recommended to her as her counsellors, and the thought that she should never be able to choose the best advisers, if her father had been so mistaken in his, made her burst into tears. It was this circumstance that Byron so pungently commemorates in the following lines: —

"Weep, daughter of a royal line,
  A sire's disgrace, a realm's decay;
Too happy, if each tear of thine
  Could wash a father's guilt away."

When the allied sovereigns were in London, after the battle of Waterloo and the capture of Paris, the Princess Charlotte appeared at court, in all the splendor of her position, as heir to the throne, and all the beauty of youth, with a well-developed form, handsome features, and a finely shaped head well set on her shoulders. She was eighteen years of age, and a desirable marriage must be sought for her. The Prince of Orange was a suitor, highly favored by the Regent and all his family, but he did not please the Princess, and the affair was in suspense, when the Duchess of Oldenburg, sister of the Emperor of Russia, resolved to prevent that alliance. She wanted the house of Orange to be connected with Russia, by a marriage with a Russian princess, and she contrived to have the young Prince made so in-intoxicated at a court ball, that when he danced with the Princess Charlotte, he completely disgusted her, and she resolved that night she would never marry him.

That one surrounded as she was by court etiquette and Tory influences, dictated to by a heartless father, and watched over by an unfeeling grandmother and aunts, should be able to make a love-match, was very extraordinary, and I can only attribute it to a kind Providence, who sent her this great blessing to make up for all the bitter trials of her childhood. It was brought about in this way. Prince Leopold came to London with the allied sovereigns, and was the bearer of a letter to Princess Charlotte, from a friend of hers on the Continent, who instructed him to ask for a private interview, and deliver the missive himself. This he did, and that first interview established a sympathy between them which soon ripened into love. Before asking the Princess in marriage, of her father, he returned to Paris, made his proposals from there, and had them approved and recommended to the Regent by some of the royal personages about him.

He was soon allowed to return to London, the accepted lover of the Princess; and then began that happy life which continued unabated through the rest of her short career. To one who had never known the endearments of family ties, had never poured out her feelings to a mother or sister or brother, and was allowed very few intimacies, this heart-union with a true and noble character, this tenderest of all affections, this outpouring of the inmost feelings to a sympathizing soul, must have had peculiar charms, and made her the happiest woman in England.

The whole nation appeared to rejoice in her

happiness. Statesmen of all parties approved of the alliance. Persons of all classes exulted in its being a love-match; and she looked forward to her marriage as the means of delivering her from much of the etiquette and formality of the court, which had always been so distasteful to her.

When they were discussing in Parliament what her income should be, and some speeches made which rendered it probable that it would be less than had been expected, she said, "If they will not give us enough to live as Prince and Princess, we will live as Mr. and Mrs. Leopold, and I shall like that quite as well."

Princess Charlotte had always wished that she had been born the daughter of a nobleman, and envied those whom she knew, their free country life on their paternal estates. She therefore resolved that her future residence should be far enough from London to afford her rural pleasures. Accordingly, the handsome estate of Claremont, in the parish of Esher, in the beautiful county of Surrey, was purchased for her, and met all her wishes. The house had been long unoccupied, and numerous workmen were employed in making it fit for a royal residence. The porter's lodge had been rented for a dame's school, and the old woman who kept it was greatly troubled at being obliged to quit the premises. In answer to the Princess's numerous inquiries about all that was going on at Claremont, she was told this, and she immediately said, "The poor old soul must not be turned out. If she will give up her school she may remain and be my porteress." To all the remonstrances of her courtly friends on the necessity of having a man for her porter, and the want of style in having an old woman to open her palace gates, she turned a deaf ear; and the next time she drove down to Claremont she made the dame very happy by telling her she might remain in the lodge. A faithful gate-keeper she proved, for having received orders to admit no visitors without a pass from a gentleman in the village who was appointed to give them, she refused to open the gates for a royal duke, because he had no permit. In vain he told her that he was uncle to her mistress, and had a right to go in. She would not let him pass; and he humored her by sending an outrider for the required ticket, and chatting with her the while. On hearing this account of her old woman the Princess was delighted, and exulted in her choice of a female porter.

The marriage took place in Carlton House, and was as private as the Princess could make it. She went down to Claremont as soon as it was over, and, by a secret arrangement of hers and a sudden departure from the palace, she escaped having two maids of honor in the same carriage with herself and Prince Leopold. A gentleman who saw her, as she passed out of the court before Carlton House, told me that she was laughing heartily at the success of her plan for being *tête à tête* with her husband on their drive to their new home.

I had friends in Esher with whom I used to stay weeks at a time, and there I always heard interesting anecdotes of the royal pair at Claremont, all showing how rationally and happily they spent their time. The old dame at the lodge furnished one amusing incident. The Prince and Princess were fond of long evening walks, and having rambled through their own woods till they came to a gate which opened on the high road, they passed through it and returned through the village to their own front gates, and passed through the smaller opening for foot-passengers, leaving the gate open behind them. The old porteress seeing them pass supposed them to be some part of the household, but had no idea of who they were; so she called after them to come back and shut the gate. The Princess enjoyed the mistake, obeyed the command, and told of it as a good joke. The poor old dame soon heard of it and was in great trouble about it. The next day the Prince drove his wife down the avenue in a curricle with a pair of gay horses. When they approached the gateway, out ran Goody and plumped down on her knees in the middle of the carriage-way, with uplifted arms imploring pardon. The Prince called out, "Get out of the way; you frighten the horses." The Princess made him stop whilst she received the apologies which the poor old woman addressed to "my Lady Princess ma'am"; these three titles she always gave her, which so amused her royal mistress, that she would not allow of her being corrected.

In one of their long walks the happy pair found in a corner of their domain which they had not before visited, a nice little cottage inhabited by the widow of a former gardener on the place. They seated themselves in her little kitchen and talked with her without her knowing who they were. She said there was a rabbit warren near there, and she did long to catch some of them, for there was nothing she loved so much as a rabbit pie. The Prince told her he would come and shoot some rabbits for her; she begged him not to do that, for it would be robbing the grand folks up at the big house. The Princess observed that the open Bible on the table was very old and worn, and the type small and indistinct; so the next evening she drove there in her pony-chair and carried her a large new Bible, very clearly printed. When she gave it to her, she told her to look first at a certain chapter in Genesis, and drove off. She had put there a five-pound bank-note.

Prince Leopold often amused himself with shooting the game on his estate, and the Princess would accompany him and bag the birds and carry them herself. He visited the warren and shot some rabbits for the good widow. By the time he carried them to her she had found out who he was, and was much pleased to receive them from him.

Princess Charlotte had a fancy to taste one of the poor woman's rabbit pies ; so she asked her to come to her house and make one for her. This was a very alarming request, and I have heard the widow tell how she dreaded going to the great house ; what fear she had of all the fine servants there, and how, though they were very civil to her, she knew they were laughing at her homely ways. She said she was so "flustered" she hardly knew what she was about, but she managed to make the pie, and her Royal Highness said it was very good.

I was one of many strangers who visited this widow, after the death of Princess Charlotte, on purpose to hear these anecdotes. They show forth the goodness of her heart, and account for the ardent love with which she inspired all around her.

The Princess Charlotte was naturally high-tempered, passionate, and wilful, and it had always cost her a great deal of self-discipline to submit to the authority exercised over her, by so many people as helped to govern her; but when she came under the dominion of love, she found it easy to yield to the will of one whose interests were identified with her own, and whose character commanded her esteem and reverence. All who know her disposition were surprised to see her so docile and amiable towards her husband, and only one instance is remembered of her ever resenting his control, and that was an ebullition of temper that passed away very quickly, and never was repeated. It happened thus.

A greenhouse was to be built near the house, and several plans were submitted to the inspection of the Princess. She chose one that cost far more than either of the others. The Prince advised her to have a less expensive one, saying, he could build that now, without exceeding his income, but if she chose to have the more costly one, they must wait till another year for it, as he was resolved to live within his income. This affronted the Princess, and she declared that if she could not have the one she liked, she would have none. This was just before dinner, and she was evidently out of humor during the meal. At last she sent her plate to the Prince, saying, "I will take some of your dish, if you can afford it." He was shocked, but said nothing. It was his custom, when the ladies left the table, to hand the

Princess into the drawing-room, and converse with her a few minutes before returning to the dining-room; this day, he handed her out in silence, made a low bow, and left her immediately. She burst into tears, and retired to her most private apartment.

When the gentlemen came into the drawing-room, the Prince observed her absence, and went directly in search of her. At the end of half an hour, they reappeared on excellent terms with each other, and the less expensive greenhouse was built that year.

One of the Princess's funny speeches came to me very direct. She said, the Prince had cured her of two antipathies, one was to a boiled leg of pork, and the other was to her grandmother.

I cannot think the cure was very perfect, for when the Queen sent her a beautiful lace baby-cap, she put it on the end of a poker, and thrust it into the middle of a coal fire. When the Queen offered to be with her at the time of her confinement, her presence was absolutely refused. To conceal the mortifying fact, the Queen was immediately ordered by her physician to drink the Bath waters, and away she went to that city, which was a hundred miles from London, and there she remained till after the death of the Princess.

Very pleasant is it to me to recall all I have

known of the life of this beloved Princess, but to tell of her confinement and death is a painful task, believing, as I do, that she was sacrificed to the vanity of her accoucheur and the ignorance of the ladies around her. Had she been a peasant's wife, she would in all probability have lived to be a happy mother.

It had always been customary for two accoucheurs to share the responsibility of a royal birth, but the vanity and ambition of Sir Richard Croft, made him request to be the only one employed, and when it proved a very protracted labor, he was so weighed down by the responsibility he had assumed, as to be wholly unequal to the exigencies of the case. No one thought of sustaining the Princess's strength either by food or stimulants, and soon after she was delivered of a still-born child, she sank away into the arms of death.

Her previous good health and fine spirits, had prevented any one from feeling any apprehensions of the approaching crisis, and the news of her death came like a thunder-clap upon the nation. One wail of sorrow went through the land. Never was a royal personage more universally regretted, or more deeply lamented. No need of orders for a *general mourning;* the poorest laborer wore some badge of it, and in all public assemblages nothing but black was seen. It was put on, too, on hearing of her death, instead of waiting till she was buried.

The afflicted husband tried to escape from the forms of court etiquette, and all the heartless ceremonials which belonged to the occasion, by shutting himself up in her favorite sitting-room, where they had passed together their last happy hours, and when obliged to quit it, he locked the door and kept the key, lest something of hers should be moved. Her hat and cloak were on a fire-screen, just where she had thrown them on returning from her last walk, and when I visited the house, twelve months after her death, that room was still shut up, and nothing in it had been removed.

She was, according to custom, buried at midnight, by torchlight, and I well remember sitting up in my bed to listen to the tolling of the parish bell, on that night, when all the other church-bells throughout the United Kingdom were sending forth the same solemn tones. She was buried in St. George's Chapel, Windsor, and the coffin was let down slowly through the floor into a vault underneath. Prince Leopold, as chief mourner, was seated at the head of the coffin, and was so absorbed in grief, that he did not perceive that they were lowering the coffin, until he raised his head and found it gone. A brother of mine was watching him at the time, and said the start he

10

gave, and the gesture of abandonment to sorrow, were most expressive and touching.

That same brother set on foot a subscription for a national monument to the memory of the Princess. No one was allowed to give more than a guinea, so as to make it the people's doing, and the result of that contribution is the grand monument to her memory in St. George's Chapel.

CHAPTER XXV.

HANNAH MORE'S CONVERT.

WHEN I was a young girl, I was constantly hearing the praises of Miss Hannah More. Everybody had read, or was reading, her religious novel of "Cœlebs in Search of a Wife," and I used to listen with interest to the accounts given of her great popularity among the wits who flourished at the close of the last century and the beginning of this. I heard, with wonder, of her being the intimate friend of the great actor, Garrick, the favorite companion, the petted darling, of the great moralist, Dr. Johnson, and an honored member of a select literary club, jocosely called *le bas bleu*.* She was also the author of a tragedy called "Percy," which had a great success in London, and once had the pleasure of seeing Mrs. Siddons perform in it, whilst Garrick sat beside her, delighted both with the play and its author.

Miss More made one of a circle of highly cultivated, refined, and amiable persons who knew

* From the color of the stockings of Admiral Boscawen, who was one of its members.

how to enjoy each others' society in the best manner, and her letters from London to her sisters in Bristol, give a charming account of her easy intercourse with the highest nobility, the greatest statesmen, the most gifted artists, the best writers, in prose and verse, of both sexes, with many delightful persons of fine conversational powers and perfect hostesses, who knew exactly whom to bring together, and how to make the most of their guests' talents and graces. It seemed to me afterwards, on reading the Life of Miss More, by Roberts, that there never was before, and never has been since, such a brilliant society as that in which she moved as one of its greatest ornaments, loved and caressed by all. Besides this circle of *beaux esprits*, who were her intimate friends, she was occasionally drawn into the vortex of fashionable life, and unwillingly made one in the crowded assemblies of the great. The follies and vices of the gay world could not escape her observation, and she had the moral courage to attack them in a little work entitled "Thoughts on the Manners of the Great."

At the time when I first heard of Hannah More, she had retired from that brilliant society which she had so long enjoyed, and was devoting her time and talents to the improvement of the world in Christian morals. The extensive circulation of Cœlebs prepared the public to receive with favor her succeeding works, "Practical Piety," and "Christian Morals," in which she employs all the fascination of her style to recommend to the rising generation the strictest life of self-denial, and the carrying of religion into all the details of daily conduct. Vast numbers of young people profited by her lessons, and even those who thought her ethics too severe, were nevertheless made better by them. I will mention a signal instance of this in one whom I knew intimately in her mature years, and from whom I learned the facts.

Caroline Ford was the only child of a rich West Indian planter, and came with her parents to England at the age of sixteen. She was placed for two years at a fashionable boarding-school, near London, and then carried to Bath, during the season of gayety there, and brought out at a Master of Ceremonies' ball. The handsome heiress soon became the reigning belle of the season. Numerous lovers followed her steps, and the offers of marriage made to her and her father were so frequent, that to be refused by Miss Ford became a joke among her beaux, and every one of her admirers was expected to try his fate. Satisfied and happy in her brilliant *début*, surrounded by novel pleasures, and full of engagements, her acquaintance with each of her lovers was too slight to make any impression on her heart, and she was firmly resolved never to marry without being in love.

When the Bath season was over, Mr. Ford's family returned to London, where they had formed a large circle of acquaintances, and anticipated another brilliant career for their daughter; but it was ordered otherwise. She had enjoyed the sunshine of prosperity, and was now to be tried by adversity. The appalling news came that the agent, in whose hands Mr. Ford had left all his property in Jamaica, had absconded, taking with him all that he could appropriate. The plantation remained, of course, and the owner found it necessary to return immediately to it. Mrs. Ford readily decided to accompany her husband, but she could not bear to deprive her daughter of the chance of making a suitable match in England. So it was arranged that she should be placed, as a parlor boarder, at the same school where she had been a pupil, and the lady at the head of the establishment promised to be a mother to her. She was to accept the invitations of her mother's friends, and to be as much in society as possible. She was provided with a lady's maid, to wait upon her, make her dresses and take care of her wardrobe; and this maid was also to accompany her mistress wherever she went in a hired carriage. She was at first so much depressed by the absence of her parents and the entire change in all her surroundings, that she could not avail herself of the kindness of the friends who invited her to their houses. She had the company of three young ladies, who were parlor-boarders like herself, and they agreed to begin a course of reading together, which should be really useful to their minds. While they were doubting whether to take history or biography, Shakespeare or Milton, one of them proposed reading a new book just presented to her. It was Hannah More's "Practical Piety." The perusal of it produced such an effect on the mind of Caroline Ford that she resolved to follow her parents to Jamaica, and give up the life of ease and gayety which they had provided for her. She felt it to be her duty to share their adversity rather than increase it by her expensive mode of life. The lady of the house admired her self-denial, but doubted whether her parents would approve of it. Finding her young friend resolved on acting up to her own sense of duty, she agreed to let her use for her outfit the next remittance sent to pay for her board. The lady's maid was now employed in making up calico dresses and such plain garments as would be useful and suitable for plantation life.

In order to avoid the opposition to her departure which she knew that the friends of her parents would make, she kept her intentions a profound secret, engaged her passage in the same packet which had brought her over from Jamaica, and when all was ready, made the journey to Southampton alone. Her funds were just enough to carry her there, but not sufficient to pay her passage. As the captain knew her father, she felt sure that he would not insist on being prepaid. She was not disappointed. One of the best berths was reserved for her; but she did not relish the behavior of the captain. He was altogether too free and patronizing, — making her feel that she was under an obligation to him.

Her motherly friend was in daily expectation of another remittance from Mr. Ford, and promised to forward it to her if it arrived before the packet sailed. All the passengers were on board and assembled in the cabin when it arrived. She showed the draft to the captain, and told him she should not pay him with it, as she owed it to a friend, who had never taken any advantage of her want of money, but freely lent her all she had needed. This hint was sufficient. It procured for her the respectful treatment she required. Her fellow-passengers were the Governor of Jamaica, with his family and suite. She was cordially received into their circle, treated as one of the daughters, and on arriving was carried to the Governor's house, and made quite at home there.

A letter from Caroline now gave her parents

the surprising news that she was near them. On hearing that she was at the Governor's, her mother advised her not to hurry home, but to prolong her stay, where she was in the best society, and might find a good match among the officers whom she would meet there. This was a sad damper to the filial feelings which had made her ask for an immediate conveyance home, and her mind was not attuned to the gay scene around her. She was much admired and caressed; the officers of the Governor's staff were devoted to her; every visitor, but one, distinguished her, and that one was the surgeon-general of the forces, — a handsome man, with good manners, but so silent and reserved as to be little known or liked. To be wholly neglected by any gentleman within reach of her fascination, was such a novelty to our heroine, that it drew her attention to Dr. Bury, and the exchange of a few words with him made her wish for more. At last he said to her, "I see you are not happy here; you wish to go home; and I will drive you there on any day you will name." If he had been her good genius, he could not have offered her a more precious boon. She gratefully accepted his kind offer, and, bidding adieu to her hospitable friends, she entered the well-appointed curricle of the silent bachelor, and a delightful drive of six hours took her to her father's plantation.

She and her handsome escort were of course well received. He was invited to stay then, and, on leaving the next day, to repeat his visit soon. He did not need urging on this point; he became a frequent visitor, and proved a welcome variety in the monotonous life of a plantation. In due time the offer of his hand and heart to the lovely recluse was joyfully accepted by the parents, and carefully considered by her. She preferred him to all other men, was much attached to him, but she feared he would not be as happy married to a woman without fortune, as he was as a bachelor. He had an income, besides his pay, but he lived luxuriously, and spent it all. If he married her, he must provide for new expenses, and deny himself his old indulgences. How would he bear that? She told him frankly all her doubts and fears. These he combated, as a lover would, and succeeded in convincing her that his happiness would be greatly augmented by marrying her. She accepted from her mother a substantial, but very plain outfit; and she told me that the very fine ladies of Kingston were much shocked by her appearing as a bride in a plain straw bonnet, with white ribbons. Colonial ladies are so afraid of not keeping up with the fashions of the parent country, that they are apt to go to extremes, and they were astonished to see one so lately from England in such simple attire. She so arranged her mode of living that her husband's income proved sufficient for them, without his being aware of any sacrifice of personal indulgence. Her talent for thrifty management increased as fast as her family enlarged, so that with three young children, she spent no more than when first married. Before the fourth child was born, Dr. Bury had sold his commission, taken his family to England, and established himself in Bath as a practising physician. It was there that I first knew them. She was still very handsome, and was performing her duties as a wife and mother in a most exemplary manner.

There was at that time an excellent opening for Dr. Bury to become a successful practitioner in Bath. The most fashionable physician had run wild on the subject of natural philosophy, denying the existence of caloric and advocating many absurdities. Another doctor had imposed upon the public by attributing every disease that came under his notice to the morbid contraction of one small muscle in the body, and had outraged common sense by his treatment of it. Nothing is too absurd for the credulity of invalids, and for a while he carried all before him, but his full-blown fame had just collapsed; his patients were ashamed of having been under his care, and were all ready to welcome a new physician with such antecedents as Dr. Bury. Unhappily this favorable juncture was lost on the military man, who had been so long in a tropical climate that his energies were all gone; he could not screw himself up to the exertion and industry necessary for success as a family physician, and his practice dwindled instead of increasing. His wife's father died before he had retrieved his fortune, and all the trials and burdens of a large family and a small income fell on Mrs. Bury. She bore them bravely, and often surprised me by the indulgence she showed for her husband's inefficiency.

When she had five boys to educate, she persuaded the Doctor to remove to the ancient town of Bedford, celebrated for its free grammar-school, founded and endowed in 1556, with eight exhibitions of eighty pounds a year each, to the universities of Oxford, Cambridge, and Dublin. Her sons did not take naturally to books, and the antiquated mode of instruction then in use at that grammar-school was not calculated to rouse their dormant faculties. They only learnt there what was never of the least use to them in after life, and they were left in ignorance of all useful knowledge. In talking with one of these boys, a lad of sixteen years old, I found that he did not know whether the sun rose in the east or in the west; but he could construe Latin.

Too indolent to make money, and too honorable to run in debt, Dr. Bury, after a long struggle with poverty, made up his mind to emigrate to Canada, and avail himself, for the sake of his sons, of the inducements to settle there held out by his government to men in his situation. I was in England when he came to this decision, and he and his two oldest boys took passage in the same packet in which my husband and I sailed for New York. We were both painfully impressed with the extreme unfitness of the trio for the life they were about to enter upon. Neither of them had read about Canada, or studied its geography to any purpose. They did not know the difference between Upper and Lower Canada, nor why they were so called, and I labored in vain to interest them in learning more about it. Dr. Bury was to make a settlement and have a house built, and then his wife was to follow with all the other children. Land was assigned to him, and he was about to improve it, when he was suddenly carried off by cholera. As soon as the news reached his wife, she resolved, though it was winter, to go directly to Canada, taking with her her eldest daughter and two other children, leaving the rest to follow in the spring, with a faithful nurse in her employ. She was impressed with the importance of joining her two sons in Canada, left, as they were, to their own guidance on losing their father; and when asked how she could leave her baby, she said, "My baby can do no wrong; my boys may." Her timely arrival prevented the land from becoming the exclusive property of the oldest son. The legal papers which were to convey the land to Dr. Bury, had not been completed, and an official, who was friendly to the Doctor, kept them unfinished until some one should appear on behalf of the widow and the rest of the family.

Here we see in the mature woman the same characteristics which marked her girlhood; the same resolute devotion to duty, the same uncompromising conscientiousness; and those, with many other Christian graces, were first called forth and fostered by the religious works of that highly gifted and truly devoted woman, Hannah More.

CHAPTER XXVI.

A CONVERTED JEW.

A CONVERTED Jew is, to me, a very interesting person, especially if his conversion to Christianity does not consist in the belief of certain dogmas peculiar to some sect of Christians, but rather in his acceptance of the Jesus Christ of the Gospels as the Messiah so long expected by the Jews. Erasmus Simon, a learned Jew from Poland, was thus converted. He became a Christian as the Jews of old did, without belonging to any particular sect. His father was a learned rabbi, with a family of sons, who, according to the custom of his people, were each apprenticed to a trade, and, when that was learned, they were allowed to prosecute any studies for which they had a strong inclination. Erasmus learned watchmaking, and then went to Edinburgh to attend law lectures. There, to the horror and disgust of his family, he became a Christian. He knew that it would separate him from his brethren, but he would not resist his own convictions; and they were so strong that he entertained hopes of converting his family, if he could gain a hearing;

but that he could not do. His father forbade him his house. He did, however, return to his neighborhood, and, on conversing with his Jewish brethren, he found several who believed in Christ, but were deterred from confessing him before men by the double persecution that would follow. For unless they joined the Romish Church, both Jews and Papists would be their enemies. This state of things determined Erasmus Simon to seek a safe asylum for Jews, converted or unconverted, offered by the United States.

He married in Edinburgh a most excellent woman, one who had always taken a peculiar interest in the Jews, and was a true helpmate to him in his benevolent project. She was a worthy daughter of her mother, who made a voyage to the East Indies in order to persuade the Bishop of Calcutta to interfere with and put an end to the burning of widows in his diocese.

Erasmus Simon was indeed an Israelite without guile, and so upright and honest himself that he never suspected evil in others. In making arrangements to come to this country, he was shamefully imposed upon. He took passage in a Dutch merchantman, without any decent accommodations for passengers, had a long voyage, and he and his wife were half starved on bad provisions. Arrived in New York, they presented their letters of introduction, were kindly received, and encouraged in their design of forming a settlement for converted Jews. They found a society already established there for the purpose of converting the Israelites, and were advised to act under its auspices.

It was proposed that Mr. Simon should make an extensive tour in the Northern States, call meetings, and set forth the sad condition of those Jews in Poland who were ready to embrace Christianity, but dared not do it there. He was to unfold to his hearers his anti-sectarian views, and his plan of buying land and forming a self-supporting settlement on it for converted Jews, and contributions were to be taken up for this purpose.

It was while he was on this tour that I became acquainted with him and his wife, at New Bedford, where they spent a week at my grandfather's house, and proved very interesting guests. The simple faith of this Israelite was much approved by the Quakers there, and they contributed liberally to his scheme. He remitted the money he collected to the Society for the Conversion of Jews, in New York, for safe keeping; and when he had raised a sufficient sum, he was proceeding to buy land, and was expecting to organize a colony of Jews on the basis he had proposed; but this was not to be. The Society who held the money was resolved that the converted Jews from Poland should accept their creed, and be governed by rules of their making.

It was not in the nature of Erasmus Simon to contend for his rights. Chagrined and disappointed, he gave up his cherished scheme, and left the Society to do as they pleased with the funds he had raised.

He had now become much interested in the Indians of North America, and a pamphlet, written by Elias Boudinot, called "The Star in the West," had convinced him that they were the lost ten tribes of Israel, and he resolved to go among them and see if he could find anything Jewish in their traditions and customs. He and his wife took up their residence on the outskirts of civilization and in the midst of Indians. He preached the Gospel to them, and she fed and clothed six Indian boys and taught them to read the Bible.

Some of the natives around them had become farmers, and raised corn and vegetables. One of these was known to Mrs. Simon, and she found him a very interesting character. She was therefore shocked to hear that a company of strolling players had enlisted him in their number, to act an Indian part at a town twelve miles off. Mr. Simon was not at home, but his energetic wife drove off to that town, found her man, persuaded him that it was a degradation to act with those players, and asked what he was to receive for doing it. He said a suit of clothes at the end of the season. She told him that if he would return with her, and promise never to turn actor, she would give him a suit of clothes that evening. He did so, and she gave him her husband's clothes, at which the poor Indian was delighted; and, rubbing his hand all over his heart, he said, "All here tank you, missus."

After a few years thus spent, urgent business recalled them to England; and in London Mr. Simon hired a room, in which he used to preach to the Jews. Several were converted, and he made their being willing to learn and practice shoemaking a test of their sincerity. Both of these excellent and devoted Christians were willing to live in the humblest way, and eat the plainest food, in order to have the means of helping their Israelitish brethren.

CHAPTER XXVII.

EDINBURGH.

AMONG my pleasant recollections of a short visit to Edinburgh with my husband, is the making the acquaintance of Mr. Combe, the phrenologist, and his handsome wife. They responded most kindly to our letter of introduction, gave us a dinner, and invited several artists to meet us.

As we were strangers to the whole party, conversation did not flow readily on our first sitting down to table. After a pause, Mrs. Combe said to me, "Have the Americans forgiven my impertinent cousin for her book on their country?" I suppose that I looked puzzled, for she added, "Fanny Kemble is my cousin." I replied that she had made her peace by marrying an American, and was very popular as Mrs. Butler; and asked if she were Mrs. Combe's cousin on the Kemble side. On this she drew herself up, and looking at a picture, over the fireplace, of Mrs. Siddons, as Queen Catherine, she said, in a tragic tone worthy of her descent, "Mistress Siddons is my mother." Her manner made me feel as if it were a sin not to have known that fact, and I was silenced for awhile. But soon a gentleman drew out Mr. Combe on his favorite subject, and he entertained us with anecdotes of Spurzheim and Sir Walter Scott, and told of the growth of heads after maturity. An allusion was made to an attack on him in a review, on which he said, "The reviewers have been firing away at me for twenty years, and I mind them now no more than the Castle rock does the wind." Some one observed that his books had a wider circulation than any review, and that was answer enough.

When the ladies retired, we found Dr. Andrew Combe, author of "Principles of Physiology," in the drawing-room, and I had an interesting conversation with him. Mrs. Combe showed me a bust of Charles Kemble, modelled by her mother, and said the art of modelling had been a valuable occupation to Mrs. Siddons after she retired from the stage. Mrs. Combe regretted that an early promise of her mother had obliged her to give to Mr. Campbell the materials for her mother's biography, adding, "He was not the right man to do it." A fine picture of Mrs. Siddons, as Zaïre, was in the drawing-room, and the resemblance of the daughter to the mother was very strong, — the same commanding appearance, the same carriage of the head. Mrs. Combe told me that she and her husband were not in society in

Edinburgh, for, what with party-spirit in politics and religion, and the odium thrown on phrenology, they were almost proscribed people, being obnoxious on every account to those who ruled the world of fashion. From the elegance of their establishment, either she or her husband must have had a good fortune, and this, with her personal charms and accomplishments, might have induced even fashionables to visit her.

We met a party of very pleasant people at the house of Mr. Murray, the Lord Advocate, and among them Captain Basil Hall, the traducer of the Americans. I was pleased to observe that his manners were as rude and eccentric in his own country as they had been in the United States. He said to Mr. Farrar that he was in a very bad humor when he visited America, and did not do justice to the country. A poor excuse, but a proof that he considered an apology necessary. He told us that Dr. Chalmers was to preach at a certain church the next day, and that we must go and hear him. He gave us minute directions how to get good seats, and urged it upon us that we must go very early. We followed his instructions, and were well placed in a very crowded church, where many were obliged to stand through the whole service. After waiting nearly an hour, we saw the reverend gentleman walk quickly up the pulpit stairs between two rows of ladies seated on them. He was of middle stature, square built, with light florid complexion and hair partly gray, about sixty years of age. His appearance was prepossessing, and I expected to be much pleased. My chagrin was therefore great when he read the hymn and I found it impossible to understand him. His voice was almost inaudible from hoarseness, his articulation indistinct from loss of teeth, and a broad Fifeshire accent made his language seem like a foreign tongue. The singing of that hymn was delightful. Of the prayer I understood a little, and it was unlike any that I ever before heard. By the time he came to the sermon the power of his voice increased, and I was able to understand most of it. The object of the discourse was to raise funds to defray part of the expense of building a new church in the old town, that the seats might be let at low rates to poor families. He treated it as if he were recommending a home mission among the poor. He insisted very much on the need there was of carrying the Gospel to the poor, and not waiting for them to come and seek it; on the thankful and courteous manner in which the poor always received such messengers; and set forth the witness in every man's breast as ready to respond to the witness in the Bible, just as the two parts of a broken cleft correspond to each other.

There were many forcible thoughts in the discourse, but these were reiterated so often as to become tedious. I did not like the general tone of feeling in which he spoke of "the common people," and described the "moral picturesque" of religion in a poor man's house. It was Tory condescension, not the equality of Christianity. His efforts to be emphatic were so violent as to be distressing to witness, and the effect was that of a picture without any shadow, for he was equally emphatic in every part. He rolled about in his pulpit, and threw himself over the side of it, in a way that was very distasteful to me. The whole performance of an hour and a quarter long was tedious to me; but as that large audience was very quiet and attentive, I suppose it was interesting to them. When I compared this sermon with the last I heard in New England, I was satisfied that Dr. Channing was a far greater preacher than Dr. Chalmers.

CHAPTER XXVIII.

SALT MINES.

TRAVELLING is one of the few pleasures of this world that does not perish in the using. Southey said, "It is more delightful to have travelled than to travel," and I think he is right. The most prosperous journeys have their anxieties and disappointments, and sight-seeing is so fatiguing as sometimes to destroy all enjoyment; but in retrospect, all that was unpleasant is forgotten, and we only live over the most delightful part of our experiences. Among many agreeable recollections of a journey in the Tyrol, nothing is more prominent than a visit to the salt mines of Hallein, a few miles from Saltzburg. These mines run through a mountain which you ascend in a very light carriage, holding only two persons, and drawn by a pair of powerful horses up the steepest path I ever travelled on wheels. As we ascended, the view behind us became very grand, but I hardly dared to look at it lest the turning of my head round should drag the carriage back or tip the horses over upon us, so nearly perpendicular was the road. We stopped suddenly at a small house, and to our surprise we found ourselves at the entrance to the mines. Our party consisted of two American ladies, a young Englishman, my husband and myself. Our lackey had preceded us, to order the necessary preparations, and when he met us I hardly knew him, so much was he disguised by the white linen suit he had put on over his own clothes. He handed us over to a woman in waiting, who showed us into a little room, where we saw three suits of white linen jackets and trousers. We supposed that they were for the gentlemen, and asked for the coverings that ladies wear. What was our astonishment when she showed us by intelligible signs that this was to be our disguise! We protested in vain against the trousers. The Emperor had given strict orders that no one should enter the mine without them. The Empress herself had worn them, and so had the Princesses. This authority was indisputable; so we submitted, but not before one lady proposed giving up the sight rather than wear the trousers. This could not now be done. The carriages that had brought us up the mountain had returned, and our own vehicle had gone round to the other side to take us up when we emerged. Mrs. G—— sat down first, and suffered the woman to put her feet into the large, coarse trousers and tuck into them her travelling dress and all her petticoats. These encumbrances so increased her naturally rotund appearance, that she looked like the caricature of a little Dutchman, and Miss A—— and I laughed so immoderately that we could not begin our toilets. At last, however, we bethought ourselves that time was precious, and began the operation. A long white jacket and a short leather apron, put on behind, with a cloth cap stuck on the top of the head, over the bonnet cap, completed our grotesque appearance. When dressed we could not stop laughing at each other and at ourselves. Miss A—— thought she never could appear before our gentlemen, but I told her there was no retreating now; she was in for the whole, and must make the best of it. Knowing that the men about the house were used to the sight, we marched boldly out before them, and saw no change in their countenances. We next met Mr. Farrar, and envied him his good looks, for the cap became him, and his white suit only made him look a little stouter. Not so our young Englishman. He looked like a fat baker or man cook, and when they both saw my figure they laughed themselves speechless. I had preceded the other ladies, and the gentlemen, having seen me first, were less affected by their appearance, and could control their mirth. Miss A—— was tall, and bore the disguise better than her companions. The cap and jacket were becoming to her, and the Englishman said that, viewed in front, she looked like a Circassian beauty, and viewed sideways, she was like a fat burgomaster. We soon entered a dim chamber of the mine; and, scarcely reconciled to our dress, we were put to a further trial, by being required to sit astride on a long wooden bench, close to each other, each holding a lighted candle. This bench, which was on wheels, was dragged along at a moderate pace through a long gallery, just large enough to admit us. Our wheels ran on wood, and on each side of us were wooden logs, through which the salt water is conveyed out of the mountain. We had not ceased to wonder at our predicament when we were allowed to dismount from our wooden horse, and found ourselves at the top of a shaft, down which we were to slide in the most curious way. Two large round poles, placed about eight inches apart, were carried from the top to the bottom of the shaft, at an angle of sixty degrees; on these we were to seat ourselves and slide down into the dark abyss below, — for our lights revealed nothing beyond the entrance. Before each lady was a miner seated on these poles, his legs extended on them; he had hold of a rope which glided through his gloved hand, by which to regulate his pace. She put her hands on his shoulders and sat on the poles as he did. We now saw the use of the aprons put on behind. That smooth black leather was to slide upon. Thus adjusted, and very carefully instructed by our valet, off we set, at a very moderate pace. I liked the motion, and soon wished to go faster. The gentlemen went down alone; and any Yankee, accustomed to coasting when a boy, would soon feel at home on these slides. This first one was two hundred feet long. It seemed but too short to me, and I was glad to hear that there were four more to be descended. We now walked a long way through very narrow galleries cut in the solid rock, stopping occasionally at some larger opening to see some part of the salt-works, or some memorial of a royal visit, or a collection of the productions of the mine, in which red salt in large transparent masses was the prettiest object, and the remains of Roman tools were the most curious.

Again mounted on the top of a slide, I felt very courageous, and told my miner to go fast; so away we sped into the dark abyss, and were down in a few seconds. Arrived at the bottom, I looked up at those on the way, and seeing the lights at the top, I could appreciate the length and steepness of the slide, and was surprised at my own fearless descent. We now walked a long way before coming to another slide, and when we had descended that, we found ourselves on the margin of an illuminated lake, which looked as black as ink, and was set round with lights in fanciful shapes. A wooden raft with seats on it received us, and we floated over this subterranean lake with barely room enough between the water and the earth over our heads for us to sit upright. This was the most extraordinary part of the whole, for the roof is composed of earth and salt, and the salt is obtained by filling up the whole space with fresh water. This eats away the roof, and the salt dissolves in the water, whilst the earth falls to the bottom. They then lead off the salt water in logs, dig out the earth, and repeat the process. Now if the roof of this place is so easily crumbled away, what prevents its falling in, and burying all under it in inextricable ruin? The effect of the illumination was very beautiful, and our passage over that dark water seemed like a dream. On leaving it, we had two more slides. One of them was five hundred feet long, but we got on it half way down. In all, we descended on slides about eight hundred feet perpendicular height, besides going down some long and steep ladders. When on these we felt the full benefit of our male attire. We could not have gone down in safety in our usual dress. As it was, we had no difficulty. When all was seen and done in these vast subterranean wastes, which employ three hundred men daily within the mountain, and two hundred without, we had to make our exit through a little gallery cut in the solid marble rock, a mile and one third in length. To do this, we again mounted what they call their wooden horse, and were drawn by miners, at a rapid rate, with a current of cold air in our faces, and in perfect silence. We had no space in which to move a limb, and were charged to keep erect and quiet, for the least motion would have brought us in contact with the rough marble wall that was flitting by us at a great rate. The time of this strange ride seemed very long. When we had advanced more than half way we saw daylight at the farther end, looking in the dark prospective like a star. When at last we reached the opening, and were ushered back to the green earth, a fine sunset, with its rose-tints, made a very striking contrast to the scenes we had left.

We paid well but willingly for our extraordinary expedition, found our bonnets, shawls, and parasols awaiting us in another dressing-room, and a woman to help us unrobe. Half an hour's walk brought us to the village of Hallein, where our carriage was waiting for us, and a drive of two hours carried us back to our hotel in Saltzburg.

CHAPTER XXIX.

NOVELLO FAMILY.

IN travelling through England at any time for the last ten years, you may have seen at every railway station a framed and glazed placard, with the words NOVELLO'S CHEAP MUSIC.

On inquiring the meaning of this, I was informed that a music publisher had brought within the reach of moderate fortunes and of professional musicians the compositions of the great masters, such as Purcell, Beethoven, Mozart, Handel, and others, hitherto published in such an expensive manner as prevented their being known to thousands capable of enjoying them. Mr. Novello was of Italian origin, but was born in England and married to a truly English wife. He was a fine performer on the organ, and had such a high relish for classical music that he desired to make it accessible to the many. His large family of children inherited his musical taste and talent, and were endowed with fine voices. Some had other talents also, and all were highly gifted. His daughter Clara has long been considered the finest vocalist in England;

and I have heard her say that she was brought before the public so young, that she thought only of satisfying her father by her performance, and paid no regard to her audience. In this way she escaped all embarrassment and never had a stage-fright. When she sang in operas, she was always attended at the theatre by her mother. After great success in England she went to Italy, and was performing in Fermo, a city near the Adriatic and within the boundary line of the Papal States. At Fermo was one of the estates of the Count Gigliucci. He was extravagantly fond of music, and was of course delighted with the performance of the lovely Clara Novello. On making her acquaintance he found she had been well educated, and that her vocal powers were her least merit. He became enamored of the woman rather than the singer, and resolved, if possible, to make her his wife. His suit was well received, and the *prima donna* of the public became his. She renounced her profession, and entered upon her duties as the mistress of a large establishment, determined to perform them so well that no one should think that her former life had unfitted her for them. She found the servants in a state of insubordination, having taken advantage of the feeble rule of the Count's aged mother, and a thorough reform was instituted by the young wife.

She had scarcely reduced everything to order, when, in 1848, the war of independence began, under the sanction of the Pope, and Count Gigliucci was chosen to represent Fermo in the first constitutional parliament in Rome, called the *Consiglio Legislativo*. Pio Nono, then a liberal, called on the patriots to furnish horses for his cavalry, and the Count was among the first to give his. When bad advisers frightened the Pope out of his liberal views, this act, with other proofs of the Count's patriotism, caused a sentence of exile to be passed upon him. He was obliged to leave suddenly, and his wife followed in their travelling carriage, drawn by oxen. They took up their residence in London, and the Countess resumed her professional career under the name, so dear to the English public, of Clara Novello.

She became the happy mother of four beautiful children, two sons and two daughters, and she arranged her affairs so well that her public duties never interfered with her private ones. No children are better cared for than hers, and no husband could have a happier home.

When the failing health of Mr. Novello obliged him to give up his business in London, he chose Nice for his residence; and it was there that I had the happiness of making the acquaintance of his family. He had lost his wife, and there lived with him then his eldest daughter and her husband, Mr. and Mrs. Cowden Clarke, and his eldest son and youngest daughter, both single and devoted to the happiness of each other. They lived in a villa about a mile out of the town of Nice, and not far from them the Count Gigliucci and his family spent half the year.

My first call at Mr. Novello's convinced me that I should enjoy the society of his gifted children. The name of Mrs. Cowden Clarke recalled to my mind that elaborate work, the Concordance to Shakespeare, which I now found to be the performance of the lady before me. The walls of the room in which I was received were covered with pictures of great merit, the works of a brother who died at twenty-three years of age, leaving these numerous paintings to tell of his genius and his industry. A remarkable chair in this room attracted my attention. It had on its carved back a small bust of Shakespeare, in ivory, and a silver plate with an inscription, and was covered with the richest damask. I found it was an offering to Mrs. Cowden Clarke from some gentlemen and ladies in New York, as a token of their appreciation of her Concordance. The day that I called, she had just received from the Appletons, in New York, a large volume containing engravings of sixteen "World-noted Women," for which Mrs. Cowden Clarke had furnished a biography of each. She lent the book to me, and I found her letterpress far superior to the pictures.

Among the numerous works of this lady, "The Girlhood of Shakespeare's Heroines" appears to me the most original and a wonderful production of her imagination. To form a just idea of what those heroines must have been when young, from what the great dramatist depicts them in mature life, seems to me a most difficult task and very successfully accomplished.

Mr. Cowden Clarke was as true a worshipper of Shakespeare as his wife, and had been a popular lecturer in England on the subordinate characters of that author's plays.

The Novello family had a large circle of acquaintance among the inhabitants of Nice, as well as the winter visitors, and were invited to all their parties. These civilities they could not return in kind, owing to the ill health of their father; but Mr. Cowden Clarke devised a way of returning them tenfold, by having several morning receptions, in which he read his lectures to his friends, and a high treat it was. He read them with dramatic effect, and made his hearers feel that they had never before appreciated the subordinate characters of those plays.

Mr. and Mrs. Cowden Clarke have edited several editions of Shakespeare; and being admitted to their working-room, I saw the pains they took to ascertain the best reading of doubtful passages. A long table was covered with old and modern editions of the play in hand, all open at the sentence they were upon; and after careful comparison and consideration, they adopted what seemed to them the genuine language of their author. The text so chosen is now considered the best, and I have heard from them that they are preparing three editions at once, according to their chosen version.

The Countess Gigliucci was a great favorite with Queen Victoria and Prince Albert, and when the Princess Royal was to be married, they wished her to sing at a court concert. It was in the winter, which season she always spent at Nice, and when some one about the court wrote to ask her if she would not come to the Royal wedding, she declined. On hearing that she was not coming, Prince Albert asked her correspondent to tell her that he could not enjoy the concert unless he heard her voice. This compliment had the force of a command, and she made the winter journey to London, was highly appreciated by the Royal family, and returned well pleased with her excursion.

Since the deliverance of Italy, Count Gigliucci has taken possession of his estates at Fermo, and represents that place in the Parliament at Turin. Fermo has become a part of the present Kingdom of Italy. The Countess no longer sings in public, but takes her proper place among the

Italian nobility and gentry, and introduces her accomplished daughters into society. One of her sons is in the army, the other in the navy. When Nice became a part of France, the Novello family, who could not live under a despotic government, removed to Genoa, and settled themselves in a grand old palace, transformed by the judgment and taste of Mr. Alfred Novello into a luxurious modern mansion, occupying the finest situation near the city, and commanding the most extensive and beautiful views of the Mediterranean, its coasts and promontories.

CHAPTER XXX.

VOYAGES.

I HOLD in remembrance the peculiar features of nine voyages that I have made across the Atlantic, and am surprised to find on reflection the variety of the circumstances which mark each. The first one I made before it was believed that steam would ever carry a vessel across the ocean, and this sailing voyage was forty-eight days long, owing to gales in the Channel which obliged us to put into Ryde, in the Isle of Wight, and also to calms on the ocean.

Among the various incidents of this long voyage was that of a man overboard, and the exertions of a boat's crew who volunteered to go after him, at the risk of their lives, but failed to reach him. We also had the robbery of a steerage passenger's trunk, containing all his property in silver dollars. A court of inquiry was held, all the passengers had their baggage searched, but the missing silver was not found for some days. At last one of the sailors pulled it up through the bung of a water-cask, sewed up in a long, narrow piece of canvas. He had seen a man making that covering for it, so the thief was detected, tried, convicted, and put in irons. Great was the joy of the emigrant, whose sole resource was that money, with which he intended to buy a farm. Another incident of this voyage was the meanness of one of the owners of the ship, who was a passenger on board of her, and took upon himself to economize, by rolling up the cabin carpet, taking down all the ornamental curtains from the berths, and feeding us on salt provisions. The gentlemen passengers signed a "round-robin," remonstrating in strong terms against his conduct, and insisting on his leaving all power in the hands of the captain. He did so; the furniture was replaced, and we had fresh meat every day.

My next voyage was one of only twenty days, sailing smoothly over a summer sea. One strange character among my fellow-passengers remains indelibly impressed on my memory. She was a great, stout Englishwoman, the wife of a British consul in some Spanish port of Central America. She was dressed in the fashions of twenty years before, short waists and narrow skirts, which made her stout figure look as if it were stuffed into a pillow-case. She told me she was the mother of two grown-up daughters; that she had failed to make them like English girls, — they would imitate the Spanish ladies; and she was so disgusted with their ways, that she had left them and their father to their own devices, and was on her way to England, where she intended to live in a pretty cottage in Devonshire. She also informed me that she had been twice married. Her first husband was an English officer in the East Indies, much older than herself, a widower and the father of three little girls, who had been sent to England to be educated. When they were old enough to be married, she was sent by their father to bring them home, with orders to give each a handsome outfit, such as would answer for them if they were soon married. She attended to all this, and they were on their way to India, when they stopped a few days at the Cape of Good Hope, and there, she said, "I married them all." "Married without seeing their father!" I exclaimed. "O, yes; I formed very good matches for them, and when their father seemed disappointed at not seeing them, I told him he could not have married them better than I had done. 'A bird in the hand, you know, is worth two in the bush.'"

My fourth voyage was the most interesting and agreeable one that I ever took. We sailed from New York on the 1st of August, 1836, on board the *good* ship Orpheus, with the *very good* Captain Bursley, in the *extra good* company of Harriet Martineau, Lieutenant Wilkes (who has since become famous by his capture of the Trent), Miss S. T——, and Mr. S. G. W——. These, with my husband and myself, made a party of six, who enjoyed a great deal together, and were quite independent of the rest of the passengers, who were disagreeable and even hostile to our coterie. One of the best state-rooms had been engaged for Miss Martineau and her friend Miss S. T——; but on coming on board, she found her berth occupied by the niece of an old Dutch lady, our fellow-passenger. After a gentle remonstrance, Miss Martineau gave up her right to it in the most amiable manner, and took a very inferior one. The lady who had thus seized on what she had no right to never occupied the berth, but chose to sleep on a sofa in the ladies' cabin, thus enacting the part of "the dog in the manger."

Our good captain had more to do than any man I ever saw in command of a ship. He had two poor, inefficient mates, which obliged him to be continually attending to every detail of sailing his vessel. He had a stupid crew of small men; so he was often obliged to put his own hands to the halliards; he was without a cook, and the steward supplied that deficiency, while he took the burden of the cabin arrangements, and drilled his two dull waiters, as ladies do their house-servants, looking at the glasses to see that they were wiped clean, and attending to the placing of the dishes on the table. All this was done with perfect equanimity of temper. He was the *beau ideal* of a sailor, and the guardian angel of us all.

We found Mr. Wilkes a very agreeable companion, full of information and of good sense. He was going to Europe to get mathematical instruments for the expedition to the South Pole, so he and the Professor had long talks upon astronomy. An elderly Scotch gentleman often joined our party, and having lived thirty years in London, among authors and artists, he amused us with anecdotes of Sir Thomas Lawrence, Fuseli, Charles Lamb, Thomas Hood, and others. But our greatest treat was the conversation of Miss Martineau. She told us of the part she had taken in the new Poor Law Bill, the Tax Bill, and the Factory Bill; that she was consulted by the ministers and the commissioners, and bound to secrecy by them, and intrusted with documents the most private and precious. She was staying at Lambton Court, the seat of the Earl of Durham, while she was writing her Illustrations of the Poor Law System, and had, at her brother's house in Newcastle, a great trunk of papers, containing the evidence collected for the ministers, which had been lent to her for materials for her work. Finding Lord Durham and Lord Howick very desirous of knowing beforehand what the new bill was to be, she told them some of its principal features, and brought over to Lambton Court some of the evidence for their perusal, which interested them extremely. In consequence of what Miss Martineau told Lord Durham, he made an experiment of the new law on his own estate, among the colliers, many months before the bill passed, and it succeeded perfectly.

She gave us a very amusing account of her intercourse with the commissioners appointed to examine into the indirect taxes, i. e., excise duties. They wanted her to write upon *starch*, but she said she could not illustrate such a prosaic subject; it was not picturesque enough; but she was willing to write on *wine* or *glass;* and the abuses in those departments furnished a good field. As soon as it was known what subjects she was upon, persons in those trades came to her with the very information she needed. Her account of Lord A——p and the direct taxes showed how little some of the ministers knew on the subject, and how important were her notes and hints. It was the same with the Relief Bill for Dissenters. Being a Dissenter herself, she was continually applied to for information on the subject.

She told all these particulars of her intercourse with the great statesmen of the day with the same directness and simplicity that she would if speaking of a third person. She was too full of the matter to be full of herself.

I always felt, after a long talk with her, that she was a very remarkable woman, and that it was a great privilege to be in such close communion with her.

When she was consulted about the Factory Bill, she objected to all legislation about children and parents, and told the ministers so; but if that subject must be dealt with, she urged the addition of schools to the new regulations, hoping that if the bill fell through in other particulars, that clause might remain and be the foundation of a national system of education. She was employed to interest Lord Brougham in the new bill, and she did so. Commissioners were to be appointed to inquire into the abuses of factory labor for children, and Miss Martineau, who had never asked a favor for herself or any one else, now proposed to the Ministry to nominate her physician, Dr. Southwood Smith, as one of the three commissioners, because she thought him particularly well qualified for the business. This was immediately done, and he was surprised by the appointment before he knew a word about it.

Very various were the subjects of Miss Martineau's conversation. She had no desire to speak always of herself. She only did that at the request of her friends. One day she quoted some opinion of Kant's, and on some one's expressing a desire to know more of that writer, she offered to give us a lecture the next day, at ten o'clock, on the philosophy of Kant. We were all true to the appointment, and having seated her comfortably on the broad taffrail of our ship, we grouped ourselves about her and listened for an hour to her exposition of the Kantian doctrines, with great satisfaction, though not, perhaps, with as much approval of it as she felt.

I have since thought that her admiration of the philosophy of Kant may have been one of her first steps on that path which has conducted her to a disbelief of all revelation and of the immortality of the soul, — too melancholy a subject for me to dwell on here! I would rather remember her as she was, when in this country and on that voyage.

The most marked feature of my fifth voyage was my having for my fellow-passenger a learned and accomplished gentleman who belonged to the lay brotherhood of the order of Jesuits. He seemed to be learned in all languages, skilled in all sciences, to have travelled all over the civilized world, to have lived in courts and camps, to speak like an Englishman, to feel like an Italian, and yet to be pleased to call himself an American.

I was returning to the United States after an

absence of four years, with my husband in worse health than when he went abroad. The first Atlantic steamer, the Great Western, had made a few trips, but was always so crowded and the accommodations were so cramped and small, that we preferred a sailing vessel, with two large staterooms and no crowd. My husband was very ill. The man I had hired to wait on him was unfaithful and unworthy, and I was indebted to strangers for the aid I needed. No one did so much for me as this accomplished Jesuit. He spared no pains to lessen my fatigue and anxiety. He had studied medicine, and acted the part of doctor and nurse. I think I should have broken down during that voyage, had I not had his kind services.

After twelve years of suffering, my husband was sufficiently comfortable, in 1852, to allow of my paying a very short visit to my aged mother in England. A friend dined with us one Sunday, and said that if I would go, he would accompany me. On Monday I made up my mind to go, informed my friend of my resolution, and we engaged our berths on board of the steamer that was to leave on Wednesday. Among the passengers who came on board at Halifax was Mr. Cunard, the gentleman to whom we owe the most successful line of packets between the Old World and the New. He proved a very agreeable companion, and would amuse us for hours with histories of London celebrities, with whom he seemed to be familiarly acquainted. He explained to me the numerous ways in which he provided for the safety of his steamers, the extra precautions taken, and the strict discipline maintained on board of them.

We had a most propitious voyage, spent five weeks in England, and were back again in Boston harbor on the very day eight weeks that I had left.

This experience of steam navigation determined me never again to trust myself to the winds.

CHAPTER XXXI.

SWITZERLAND.

HAVING visited Switzerland at various times from youth to old age, and spent the larger part of two summers there, — one season on the Lake of Geneva, and another on that of Lucerne, — I feel intimately acquainted with the country; too much so to trust myself with writing of it here. My recollections of ten days of the finest weather, spent on horseback among the high Alps, of twenty-two mountain passes made at different times, of days spent on the Righi, and weeks at Vevay, must all be put aside. I am not writing an itinerary. I may, however, note down a few curious incidents, pleasant meetings, and coincidences, which lent a romantic interest to my journeys there.

A visit to Lausanne was made doubly agreeable by my husband's having a letter of introduction to M. de la Harpe, the venerable octogenarian, who was, in his youth, made by the Empress Catherine, of Russia, tutor to her sons. It was a very extraordinary thing for a despotic ruler to place her sons under the care of a republican, and may, perhaps, account for their being so much better than their ancestors. The Emperor Alexander I. did honor to the instructions of his Swiss tutor, and his brother Nicholas may have owed some of his good qualities to that excellent man. Judging from the animated conversation of M. de la Harpe on the subject of American slavery, he may be the original cause of the emancipation of the serfs by the reigning Emperor. We found the old gentleman living in a pretty house, set in a fine garden, though in the middle of the town. He received us most graciously, and began to talk at once on the banking system of the United States and on slavery. He treated both topics like a thinking man and a philanthropist. I turned the conversation on his own country, and congratulated him on the increased liberty of the Swiss. He responded very feelingly, spoke of the regeneration of his native land, and of his own efforts to procure trial by jury. He had fears of innovations being made too suddenly. "*Festina lente*" seemed to be his motto.

At Geneva we became interested in the Polish exiles, who had recently fled thither from fresh acts of tyranny on the part of their Austrian rulers. Their accounts of the wrongs and sufferings of their unhappy country were heart-rending, and yet we could not help listening to them, and giving to these patriots the poor consolation of our sympathy. The *valet de place* whom we employed, told me that one of these Polish gentlemen was a man of high rank, and some years ago he visited Italy in style, with his carriage and servants, and added, "I was well paid then as his guide to the sights of Naples, and now that he comes as a poor exile I wish to serve him for nothing, if you will dispense with my attendance on you."

During an excursion from Geneva to Chamouni, I happened to be at the same hotel with a Russian nobleman, who was making what was to him a novel experiment, that of travelling without his *valet de chambre* or any of his suite. He had performed the short journey from Geneva without suffering from the want of attendance, and I saw him eat as good a supper as if he had been waited upon by his own man-servant; but the next morning he came down to the dining-hall in the greatest rage, sent for the host, and upbraided him with having treated him worse than a dog; his own groom was better lodged than he had been, his bed had not been made, he had had no sheets, and he was thus ill-used because he was a Russian. The master of the inn was so astonished that he could not speak, but let his guest exhaust himself with railing; then he suddenly left the room, but returned in a few minutes, and told the Russian that there were two beds in the room he had occupied, and one was handsomely made up with sheets and pillow-cases, and begged him to come and see it. The traveller now perceived his mistake, and came to the conclusion that he had better be always under the care of his *valet*.

In Geneva I saw a collection of enamel paintings by Constantine, as beautiful as those of Bone, in London, and much more interesting, being exquisite copies of the finest pictures of the old masters, as well as some original landscapes.

These are a few of my recollections of the Lake of Geneva. Those associated with Lake Lucerne have for me an equal interest. My husband and I, accompanied by some young friends, were on our way into Italy, and passing up the lake in a steamer, where we saw a country-seat delightfully situated, at the foot of the Righi, and close to the border of the lake. I exclaimed, "How much I should like to spend next summer in that house!" A boatman told us it was a Jesuit College. We thought the Jesuits knew how to choose a fine situation. After six months spent in Italy we were again in Lucerne, and learned that the place we so much admired had long been deserted by the Jesuits, and was now just opened as a boarding-house. We immediately engaged a suite of rooms for our party of four. We found only one family there before us, consisting of Mr. and Mrs. C——, a grown-up daughter, and a son only ten years old. We sat opposite to them at table. They were civil, but not conversable. On retiring to our own apartment I said to a young lady travelling with me, "That Miss C—— is in love, and her parents do not approve of her choice." My young friend laughed at the idea of my having truly interpreted the looks of these strangers. I assured her it was so, and that before three days she would be made the confidante of Miss C——.

It happened exactly so, and we became interested in this love affair; but as the lover had no means of supporting a wife, we did not wonder at the opposition of the parents. The C——s were cultivated people, and belonged to a noble family; they were very musical, the father played on the violoncello, the son on the violin, and the ladies on the piano. We used to spend our evenings together most agreeably. We were joined in our summer residence by a family of our acquaintance from Marseilles, Mrs. R—— and her daughter, who proved a pleasant addition to our evening reunions. We ladies were all sitting round a table with our work, when Miss R—— produced her pocket-book to show Miss C—— a profile of the gentleman to whom she was engaged. The name was underneath, and Miss C—— was so startled and agitated that she was obliged to leave the room, in order to conceal her emotion. The name she saw was that of her lover, and she thought the profile was intended as a likeness of him, and that he was unfaithful to her and engaged to another. Miss R—— feared from this sudden flight that Miss C—— might be ill, so she went after her, and then an explanation took place which made both of them very happy. They were engaged to two brothers! After much persuasion, Miss C—— consented to take Mrs. R—— into her confidence, and it was well that she did so, for that lady took such an interest in the affair that she influenced her husband to provide a career for the younger brother, as he had already done for the elder one; she reconciled the parents to the match, invited them all to her house in Marseilles, and there both brothers were married to the ladies of their choice. I saw Miss C—— once after she was Mrs. M——, and we talked over together the curious combination of circumstances which had led to her happy union.

All travellers who have made the pass of the Splügen, and come down through the *Via Mala*, must have the most vivid recollection of its sublime scenery and its wonderful road. I was once walking with my husband through the last four miles of this grand pass, when we came, at a sudden turn of the road, upon a school of twenty-four boys, running, gambolling, and shouting among the rocks and precipices. Their light blouses and rosy faces gave a cheerful air to the scene, before so solemn ; and their small figures made still more apparent the immense magnitude of the objects around them. These active little creatures amused themselves in throwing down from that middle bridge, which looks as if poised in air, large masses of stone into the river far below, whilst one of their teachers counted, on his watch, the number of seconds they took in falling, and so ascertained the depth. While the boys were thus engaged, the head-master, Monsieur Töpffer, was sketching that well-known bridge which forms the prominent feature of every picture of this pass. This pedestrian party put up at the same inn that we did that night, and there we learned what a delightful relation subsisted between Monsieur Töpffer and his pupils. We made the acquaintance of two boys from New Orleans, whose parents were known to one of our party, and they told us how much they enjoyed these pedestrian journeys, and that Monsieur Töpffer wrote down every evening the events of the day, calling upon every boy to mention anything he wished to have recorded. This diary he illustrated with spirited sketches, many of them comic scenes in which the boys figured.

When we returned to Geneva we found ourselves lodged very near Monsieur Töpffer's house, and frequently saw his boys. The very *beau ideal* of a school was his; both he and his wife were loved and honored by their pupils, who extolled them with enthusiasm. They brought us former diaries of their pedestrian tours, which were printed with illustrations, and a copy presented to each boy.

Monsieur Töpffer's own ideas of education were so wise and good, that he naturally saw with great clearness the mistakes and follies of others, and he published a little book of caricature sketches, *Histoire de M. Crepin*, with pungent explanations, that ridiculed various modern systems, and were very humorous. Several other works of the same kind followed, but long after I knew him he changed his style of authorship, and made himself famous as an elegant writer of fiction. Even the Parisian critics, jealous as they are of Genevan authors, extolled the purity of his style and admired his works. His *Nouvelles Genevoises* is the most charming collection of tales that I am acquainted with in the French language, and *Le Presbytère* is one of the most beautiful and pathetic stories in any language.

CHAPTER XXXII.

A TRAVELLING COMPANION.

I ONCE had a delightful opportunity of observing the effect produced on persons of all classes and all ages by the union of beauty and goodness in a lovely young lady who travelled with me through France, Switzerland, and Italy. She was spiritually-minded, and so thoroughly imbued with the love of her fellow-beings that it shone through every act, lending a charm to all she did and said. No one could resist her fascinations, and her presence was a talisman that unlocked all doors and propitiated all officials. Often have I seen custom-house officers, addressed by her, forget their duty, and pass our luggage without examination. We travelled in Switzerland before it was full of great hotels, and used to put up at roadside inns, where the host and his family waited on their guests. These were always charmed by the beautiful and gracious stranger; they would sometimes encumber her with service in order to express their admiration, and everything in the house was put at our disposal for her sake.

On arriving in a village, she would occasionally walk out alone, and we were sure to find her surrounded by the children in the street, whom she was amusing. The little dirty creatures were interesting to her. She carried her guitar with her, and when singing to it, in a little inn parlor, I have seen the curtainless windows filled with faces pressed close to the glass outside, looking at and listening to her, while the family of our host was crowding the doorway. She had a way of treating every one as if they were of the utmost importance to her.

In cities, she was followed and pointed out as the beautiful American, and at the great theatre of San Carlo, in Milan, the attention she attracted was really embarrassing to her. In Florence, Mr. Powers was so delighted with her, that he begged to be allowed to make a portrait bust of her, in which he was very successful. She could not believe that her face deserved such a compliment, and it was with great difficulty that I persuaded her to have it done.

In Rome, our party was indebted to her charms for having the best seats at all public shows, and access to places closed to other strangers. When I was bargaining with an Italian Marquis for a suite of rooms, in Rome, I objected to his price for them as too high, and named the utmost that I was willing to give. He could not take it, but just then my young friend appeared, and in her sweet voice said, "You surely will accept the terms of Madame." He gazed at her in silent wonder and admiration, then bowed low and said, "I can refuse you nothing."

When she was presented to that interesting old man, Thorwaldsen, he was captivated by her, and on our second visit, he presented to her a bronze medal with his own head on it. We found this great artist living in the same small house which he took when he first went to Rome, though his fortunes had greatly changed. His sympathies were freely given to all poor artists, and he aided many by letting them hang their works on his walls, and when strangers came to see him, he would point out the merits of the pictures, and sometimes sell them for the needy artists. One picture which we saw there saved the life of a young man, reduced to despair by want of employment. Thorwaldsen had it hung in his parlor; it was admired, and produced so many orders that it made the man's fortune. These acts harmonized perfectly with the countenance of that fine old man, which beamed with benevolence. He looked very much like a portrait of him which I had seen in Boston, and he was quite pleased to hear that a picture of him was in the United States, as he supposed none had ever gone there. This man, whose fame has spread all over the civilized world, who was then at the head of his profession, the first of living sculptors, received all his company in a ragged old dressing-gown, put on over his drawers, and held round him to hide the absence of pantaloons. He was working on a small *bas relief* while talking to us.

In his little narrow bedroom were many precious relics. At the head of his bed was a portrait of Raphael, copied from that done by Pietro Perugino, in the Vatican; it represents him as a soldier asleep. Civic wreaths, long since faded and dried, were lying about. A bust of Napoleon I. showed that his once powerful patron was not forgotten. Very few of his own works were in his house; but in his numerous studios and workshops we saw a very large number. He had one married daughter, to whom he gave a handsome marriage portion, telling her that was all she would ever have from him, as the rest of his fortune would be left for the benefit of poor artists. We saw him once at a ball, given by the Duchess Torlonia, in full dress, which improved his appearance and made him look very handsome. He was of medium height, of rather square build, with a fair complexion, blue eyes, and flowing white locks. I stood near him when he was playing the original game of cards that was invented for the amusement of the crazy French

King. The cards were very large, and there were five suits of them, and each suit had five court cards, a knight being added to the number. What are spades with us were swords with them, — *spada* being the Italian for sword, it was corrupted into spades. Their clubs were representations of Hercules's club, and ten of them required a very large card. Tricks were taken as in whist, but it appeared to me a much more complicated game.

CHAPTER XXXIII.

WEARINESS OF ETIQUETTE.

I BELIEVE there are many minds among the votaries of fashion which are chafed and irritated by the restraints imposed upon them by the conventional society in which they are born, and such minds would often emancipate themselves, were it not that any attempt to do so is frowned down as ill breeding, or laughed at as eccentricity.

I know the daughter of an English earl who was so wearied by her training for high life that she eloped with her father's gardener, conformed entirely to her new position, and was very happy in it. She was never noticed by her family. They seemed to ignore her existence. Her husband was intelligent and industrious ; he became the owner of a valuable nursery-garden near London, exhibited his plants at the horticultural shows, and attended the dinners given on such occasions. The last I heard of him was at one of these dinners, when he was challenged to drink wine by his noble father-in-law, and did it as simply as if it had been with a fellow-gardener.

In visiting the retreat of the celebrated* ladies of Llangollen, I learned enough about them to convince me that it was a weariness of the ceremonies and restraints of high life, with a painful sense of the hollowness of worldly professions, that drove them to cut their connection with the society in which they were born, and lead a rural life among the Welsh mountains. Their disappearance from the fashionable world made a great sensation at the time, and it was generally supposed that some love affair was at the bottom of it. It was difficult to make the public renounce that idea, and the newspapers were for years inventing fictions to favor it. There was nothing remarkable in the lives they led except the privilege of doing as they pleased. There was no great scope for benevolence, but they were kind to their poor neighbors. They abridged the trouble which attends a lady's dress by wearing all the time cloth riding-habits and beaver hats. When young they rode much on horseback, when old they indulged in a carriage, and occasionally dined with a friend, at a distance of twenty miles,

* These ladies were Lady Eleanor Butler and the Hon. Miss Ponsonby, who suddenly quitted the world of fashion in London, and retired into Wales, where they spent the rest of their lives.

but always returned home at night. They were never known to sleep out of their own house, and so it was supposed that they had made a vow to that effect.

The daughters of George III. were often weary of court etiquette, and used to get rid of it by spending their mornings at Frogmore, near Windsor, a small establishment, where they enjoyed rural pleasures and were never intruded on by company. There they had their dumb pets and fed their own chickens, ran out and in unattended, and were entirely free from the trammels of royalty. I have been there just after they had left the place, and found their work and their books lying about, and everything looking like the home of a private family.

The wife of an officer in the army, who had apartments in Windsor Castle, said that the princesses would escape into her room sometimes, and beg for a glass of beer to quench their thirst, alleging as a reason for their doing so, that if they asked for it in their own home, they must wait for a barrel to be tapped, and that would cause a new office to be created, for serving beer to them between meals, and that barrel would become the perquisite of some one of the household, and a fresh barrel would be tapped every time a glass of beer was called for. So great was the discomfort of a royal household in those days. The great good sense of Queen Victoria has altered many of these things for the better.

I will here insert an anecdote of Queen Charlotte, which, though not an instance of weariness of etiquette, shows that while she was usually a slave to her own rules of form and ceremony, she could violate those of politeness and delicacy. Before there were any railroads in England, the royal family used to travel to and from Windsor in carriages and four, and Queen Charlotte would sometimes honor one of her nobility by a call in passing, and take lunch at the house. On one of these calls, she partook of some cake which she praised very highly. Sometime after the lady of the house sent a loaf of the same kind of cake as a present to the Queen. This she repeated, at the same season, every year, until she received a message from her Majesty that she should like a little more sugar in the cake. "Does she take me for her confectioner?" exclaimed the offended lady. She sent no more cake to the Queen.

A baron of high degree, in South Wales, chose a novel way of ridding himself of the form and etiquette which belonged to his rank. He determined so to ally himself in marriage that none of his aristocratic friends should be willing to visit his wife. He married a pretty and amiable milliner in the country town near his estates, had a fine family of children, and led a very happy life as a farmer. He has been seen, on a market-day, with the leaves of a fine large turnip hanging out of his coat-pocket. It was one he had been exhibiting to his brother-farmers.

CHAPTER XXXIV.

THE MAID OF HONOR. — THE ORPHANS. — THE GENERAL'S LADY.

TO any one who has read the Life of Madame d'Arblay, and remembers how irksome it was to her to fill the place of maid of honor to the Queen of George III., and how earnestly she begged her father to take her away from court, it will seem hardly credible that a young lady in the same position died broken-hearted because she was dismissed from her post of honor. But I know of such an instance, and heard from friends of the person to whom it relates, the following account.

The lady was young and beautiful, the daughter of an officer of high rank in the army, and as a favor to her father she was appointed maid of honor. The Prince of Wales was then young and handsome, and considered the most elegant man in England. Everybody at the court desired to be distinguished by him, and some of the younger ladies hoped to make him in love with them.

The heroine of my story, after being at court

for a few weeks, wrote to some friend at home that she enjoyed herself very much, that the Prince was very attentive to her, and she hoped in a few more weeks to have him at her feet. She then went on to find great fault with the German ladies in waiting, described them as cross and ugly, and showed the same aversion to them that Madame d'Arblay always felt. She closed her letter in haste, and an attendant took it while the ink of the address was still wet. It became so blotted and blurred that it could not be read, and was consequently returned to the palace to be claimed and redirected. It fell into the hands of one of the German ladies; curiosity and suspicion made her open it, and there she found ample matter to ruin the writer. She showed the letter to the Queen, who was enraged at the way in which her son was mentioned, and sending for the father of the culprit, then on duty at the palace, she put the letter into his hands, and told him to take his daughter away and never let her appear again in her royal presence. The father was much distressed, but considered his daughter's fault inexcusable and the punishment no more than she deserved. She went home, sickened and died. Her jewels and trinkets were distributed among her young friends, and the daughter of one of them gave me a garnet and gold necklace which used to grace the lovely white throat of the maid of honor, and which I still possess. The sight of it has recalled this history.

There came to Milford Haven, while I resided there, two little girls whose parents had died in the East Indies while the children were at school in England. They were brought to Milford because a brother of their father lived there, and also another distant relative, and a child was left with each of these relations. The family on whom these orphans had the least claim, treated their adopted one as if she had been their own child, and her life would have been very happy had her sister been equally well cared for. This sister was grieved for her being made a mere *drudge* in the kitchen of her uncle. He was an easy, quiet man, who left everything to his wife's management. She was a worldly-minded woman, making the best show she could on a small income, and was determined to make the most out of this unwelcome addition to her family. She dismissed one of her servants, and made her niece do as much of her work as was possible for a child of ten years old. The child was ill fed, ill clothed, and ill lodged; a more unhappy little being cannot well be imagined. Her sister was very rarely allowed to see her, because the contrast in their situations made her more miserable, or, as the aunt would say, more obstinate and stupid. The treatment of this child began to be talked about in the town, but no one had the moral courage to remonstrate with the uncle, and her condition seemed utterly hopeless, when one of those remarkable changes came to her, which we are apt to think belong only to fiction, but which I have frequently seen in my experience of seventy years. A rich aunt of these children, on their mother's side, arrived in Milford, travelling post in her own carriage, and with a man-servant and a lady's-maid in attendance. On the evening of her arrival she put up at the Nelson Hotel, and inquired of the landlady where the gentleman lived who had adopted a brother's orphan child. This led to a disclosure of the miserable condition of the niece she was in search of. She could not wait till the morning without seeing her, but drove at once to the house, which was a little way out of the town. The master and mistress were gone to a card-party. The stranger asked to see a little girl who lived there, and made her way into the house, resolved to have an interview with her. The maid-servant was in great consternation at having to send the barefooted and ragged Cinderella into the presence of such a fine lady; but it could not be avoided, and she was astonished to see the stranger embrace the child and weep over her; still more was she surprised to hear the lady tell the little girl that she would come the next day and take her away with her, and she should be her child.

The orphan who had fallen into good hands was so happy with her adopted parents, that it was thought best not to remove her; but the one who had suffered so much was carried off, educated, and brought up in a manner suited to the condition of her aunt.

A handsome young girl, the daughter of a tradesman in Dublin, married from ambition an Irish Knight, old enough to be her father, and was highly gratified by becoming Lady D——. Nor was her grief very poignant when she lost her husband, for the title remained to her, with money enough to make her independent. Her beauty and her lively conversation soon gave her many lovers, among whom she chose a general officer in the English army, who had distinguished himself in the field, and was a man of real worth. His niece was my intimate friend, and from her I learned many particulars of the General's family. He had a handsome establishment at the West End of London, and introduced his wife to a select circle of friends and acquaintances; but these did not satisfy her ambition. She aimed at belonging to the highest circle of fashionables, — a most exclusive set, who ruled the balls at Almack's rooms, and often refused to admit into their coterie ladies of the highest rank. Lady Cawdor, daughter of the Earl of Carlisle, said they would not let her belong to them, — she was not stylish enough. To penetrate this aristocratic circle was the endeavor of Lady D——'s life; but the widow of an Irish Knight could not be admitted. She would have stood a better chance without her title.

General F—— was a great favorite with George III. I remember being at a review of ten thousand troops in Hyde Park, and hearing that the King, on meeting General F——, said to him, "You feel better to-day than you did this day forty years." The General's memory was not as good as the King's. He did not recollect that it was the anniversary of the battle of Minden, at which he had held an important command, and had distinguished himself. His royal master had not forgotten it.

Lady D—— had three children, a son and two daughters, whom she educated very carefully, and brought up under the strictest discipline. It was well for them that their health was good, for she never allowed them to complain of any bodily suffering. A headache was never to be mentioned, and the word *nervous* was banished from her vocabulary. She soon married off her eldest daughter to her satisfaction; but the second one, though far more beautiful than her sister, was decidedly weak in her intellect; and when one of the most remarkable statesmen of the day began to pay her particular attentions, her mother charged her to speak to him as little as possible, never to introduce a subject of conversation, but to follow his lead, and always to listen with profound attention to what he said. This policy was successful, and the clever cabinet minister married a weak woman without knowing it.

Whenever the London season came round, Lady D—— gave what was then called a *rout*, and turned her house topsy-turvy to make it hold the greatest possible number of guests. On one of these occasions she had been exerting herself to make the most show on the least expenditure, and was rushing from room to room in the greatest *dishabille*, when a carriage full of callers drew up at her door. In a few minutes she was in an elegant morning *négligé*, seated in her boudoir, stringing pearls, and after a few minutes spent by the guests in the drawing-room, they were ushered into her presence, and she said, with the languid air then practised by fine ladies, "You find me busy; one must be so on these silly occasions; I receive company to-night, and must have my necklace ready."

This fine lady had a violent temper, and if her husband had not been remarkably calm and imperturbable, they could not have lived together.

One evening after dinner, as the family were sitting round the fire chatting, a dispute arose between Lady D—— and the General, in which he maintained his ground, and though he did it very calmly, Lady D—— was so exasperated that she threatened to leave his house forever, pulled the bell, and ordered her carriage to come to the door as soon as possible. The footman took her order, and then the General said, in the gentlest tone, "When you have done that, bring some coals to the fire." This was too much for Lady D——, she burst into tears and wept away her passion. Another victory won by the General.

CHAPTER XXXV.

PARENTAL AUTHORITY.

I KNEW a successful lawyer in Paris who was resolved to make his only son follow in his steps, share his practice while he lived, and succeed to it at his death. The son was amiable and obedient, but ere he left school he began to show a decided inclination for art. His love of music was so strong that he learned to play on the piano with extraordinary facility, and also to compose, when very young. His father approved of music as an innocent recreation, but frowned on his attempts to compose, and rarely allowed him to go to the opera. This gentle youth wrote pretty verses; his father also discouraged that. He modelled statuettes of horses and riders in clay, but they were all swept away as rubbish. Nothing was considered by the father as reasonable work, but that which his business required, and he kept his son strictly to it. A more absolute father I never knew; and while deprecating his severity, I must give him credit for having brought up his son a model of purity and uprightness, in the midst of a most corrupt state of society. This son, so strictly educated, was a highly intellectual and spiritual being, full of the finest feelings, and capable of high enjoyment from simple pleasures. He was the delight of his mother and sister. Happily for this sensitive being, he was not obliged to accept a wife of his father's choice, which would have been his fate had not very unusual circumstances led to a mutual attachment between him and a young lady who was a desirable match in the opinion of the father. An early marriage added greatly to his happiness, but did not lessen the power of his father over him. Long after he was married he could not be summoned into the presence of his father without trembling. All who know what the parental relation can be in France will understand the effect here produced by it on a very sensitive nature.

I was spending a winter in the south of France when this young couple brought me a letter of introduction from a lady in Paris. I began the acquaintance without the least idea that they were connected with anybody whom I already knew. It was therefore a mutual pleasure to discover that the youth just introduced was the son of an old friend of my girlhood. He had often heard his father speak of me, and readily adopted me as a family friend. His health had been injured by close application to office business, and his physician had frightened his father into giving him leave to spend a winter in a mild climate. It was the first vacation of more than a few days that he had ever been allowed, and he luxuriated in its freedom and leisure.

He was a great acquisition to me and my party that winter. With the simplicity and gayety of a child, he was gifted with the talents of no ordinary man. He was the life and spirit of a very genteel company of fellow-boarders in a hotel, and got up private theatricals among a set of young people who needed a world of teaching to make them act at all. He had such a talent for it that he seemed born for that vocation, and having found it difficult to get any drama that his slender troupe could act, he wrote a very clever comedy called "The Female Quixote," in which he ridiculed strong-minded women and women's rights very humorously. Besides drilling and prompting, and managing everything, he played on the piano delightfully between the acts, and when the play was over he was the very soul of wit and pleasantry. His performance on the piano was marked by taste and feeling rather than by the noisy execution so much in fashion then. His wife told me that on some grand occasion in Paris a musical composition of his was the favorite piece.

Never before had this busy lawyer had the disposal of his own time, nor so much leisure to indulge his tastes, and he improved it to the utmost. He now took to modelling with great zest, and used the studio of an artist who was perfectly amazed at the work of one who, he thought, had come to learn of him. This amateur sculptor made a beautiful equestrian statuette, and when I regretted that I could not carry away a plaster cast of it, he made a very pretty *bas relief* of a horse and had it multiplied in a composition that would bear transportation. I took the copy he gave me to Florence, and showed it to the best sculptors there, one of whom said, "The man who could do that, should never do anything else but model." They were astonished to hear that it was done as an amusement by a successful Paris lawyer. "Tell him," said another artist, "that he may be the greatest lawyer in the land, and his name will never live after him; but if he excels in sculpture, he will be immortal."

CHAPTER XXXVI.

THE VILLAGE APOTHECARY.

THE English apothecary of forty years ago was often a man ignorant of the first principles of the healing art, who passed from the use of the mortar and pestle, in his employer's shop, to the dispensing of drugs to the sick. This class of men no longer exists; they have given place to the medical practitioner, who is obliged to study medicine and pass an examination before he is allowed to prescribe as a medical man.

It is more than forty years since I passed a winter in Devonshire with an old friend, and heard that her most companionable visitor was the village apothecary. Seeing my surprise, she told me that he had been in the Guards, and went to Spain as surgeon to a dragoon regiment, and was thus thrown into the most polished society. From another admirer of this uncommon apothecary I gleaned the following history:

In the Peninsular War he received a wound in his leg, which made him lame for life, and he took this so to heart that it made him shun society while in Spain. But much worse trials awaited him on his return home. His wife, with whom he had lived very happily for many years, —his pride being continually gratified by the attention which her beauty and conversational powers attracted,—was a complete piece of deception, and having ventured too far on his credulity, was entirely unmasked. She had been dreadfully extravagant during his absence, and knew not how to clear herself of debt before his return; so she laid an ingenious plot for swindling, was detected and prosecuted. The consequences involved her husband still deeper in debt, and on his return these embarrassments, with his shame and grief, led him to bury himself in an obscure village, and by an unremitting attention to his profession, endeavor to extricate himself with honor from the pecuniary part of his difficulties.

What induced his detestable wife to inflict the next trial he never told. After a lingering and unaccountable illness, he discovered that he was laboring under the effects of *poison*, which his wife was administering, a little at a time, in almost everything he took. As soon as he admitted a suspicion of the fact, he sent for her brother, who was also a medical man, and they proceeded to analyze some coffee which his wife had just presented to him, with the most endearing persuasions to drink it. A quantity of arsenic was clearly discovered. Just then she entered the room. He broke forth in a paroxysm of rage and anguish, and ordered her never to appear in his sight again. She retreated to her mother's apartments (an old lady who lived with them, and was seldom able to leave her room,) and there the poor criminal had lived for nearly three years when this account was given to me. She was as effectually confined by fear and shame as if she had been under lock and key. She knew her life was in his hands, but relied entirely on his humanity. He knew that his was not safe a moment, but could not bear to drive her from the shelter of his roof.

It sometimes appeared a mere fable to me that a murderess lived so near to my friend's house, and that the refined, romantic man, whose conversation afforded us so much pleasure, had been driven from society by such undeserved disgrace, such tragic circumstances. He seemed to dread everything that could remind him of his former happiness; the contrast was too strong to be endured. When we remonstrated with him for neglecting literature, and urged him to embellish his retirement with some of its best productions, he replied, "No, I must not, I cannot, I am afraid of being in love with the world again. Since I have buried myself here it has been my study to deaden every feeling, every taste, and to become, if possible, a mere machine."

CHAPTER XXXVII.

THE GARDENER'S GRANDDAUGHTER.

WHEN Napoleon I. threatened to invade England, and dictate terms of peace from St. James's Palace, a very large militia force was added to the standing-army of the country, and men of all classes cheerfully enrolled themselves in the regiments of their different counties. The drilling was as thorough as that of the regular army, and the discipline as strict. They lived in barracks, and their quarters were frequently changed, to make them more of soldiers and less of citizens. Many fine ladies left luxurious homes and lived either in lodgings in some country town or in the officers' quarters, in the barracks. It was well for those regiments whose officers had their wives with them, for where there was no female society the manners and the morals of the young men were apt to degenerate.

A gentleman whom I knew when he was in middle-life, told me of his experiences when he entered the militia, a stripling of eighteen, as first-lieutenant. He was the youngest officer in the regiment, and was both the plaything and the victim of his comrades. He was sometimes made to sit on a chair in the middle of the mess-table, after dinner, and drink wine with every one present, until, quite tipsy, he was borne off to his bed. He was much displeased at being so treated, but did not know how to help himself. One day he left the mess-table before the dinner was over, and walked out of the town into a neighboring wood, on purpose to avoid being made to drink wine. Much pleased at having thus foiled his tormentors, he walked on briskly until he came upon a group of young people, which he stopped to admire. Among some hazel bushes was one higher than common, and in its branches was a little boy gathering the nuts and throwing them into the apron of a very pretty girl, who was holding it up to receive them. A slight but well-rounded figure was shown to advantage by her attitude, while her head, thrown back, prevented her luxuriant curls of light hair from hiding her large blue eyes and fair complexion. A small aqueline nose, well-cut lips, and the whitest of teeth, completed her charms. She was a study for a painter. Though no artist, the young lieutenant was transfixed with admiration of this rustic beauty. She and her companion were so engrossed by their nut-picking that they did not observe the stranger, who watched them from a distance, until they had filled their basket and were going off with it. He then joined them and entered into conversation with the girl. She answered his questions, and put some to him, in a simple, artless way, that well became her. He accompanied her to her home, a neat little cottage surrounded by flowers and vegetables, and left her at the garden-gate. That one interview shaped all his future life. He became extravagantly in love with this Ellen Potter, the gardener's granddaughter; he wooed and won her clandestinely, for she never allowed him to make the acquaintance of her grandfather, knowing that he would forbid any young officer to visit her. Many were the meetings in the wood, and many were the hours spent in the old man's house, when he was absent working in other people's gardens.

Lieutenant B—— was an orphan, and heir to a small fortune. His guardian gave him a handsome allowance, and that with his pay would support two as well as one; so he resolved to marry the girl of his heart, but to keep it a secret until his regiment should be ordered elsewhere. His brother officers soon discovered that he was in love, but never supposed that he would marry a peasant girl; they thought he was only amusing himself, and they were satisfied with cracking their jokes upon him. Ellen was such a mere child that she knew not the importance of the act when she went to church with her lover and was there married. She did it to please him, and that was enough for her. On returning home she put her wedding-ring in her pocket, and went about her work as usual.

When news came that the regiment was to move into a distant county, Ellen's marriage must be disclosed to her grandfather. He commanded her respect and veneration, and she dreaded to tell him what she had ventured to do without consulting him. She has described to me the scene when she and her husband stood before the old man and confessed that they were married; and I wish I could remember *verbatim* the words of her grandfather, for they were full of wisdom and of concern for her future happiness. He was not angry; he was only sorry for the mistake his beloved Ellen had made.

The young officer had fancied that his alliance with a peasant girl was an honor conferred on the gardener, but what he now heard made him regard the connection very differently. He was humbled, and promised the old man to do everything in his power to protect his wife in the new position in which he should place her.

He obtained leave of absence, and did not join his regiment for several weeks, during which time his bride was properly equipped as an officer's lady, and learned many things necessary to her new position. She was by nature refined and polite; her perceptions were quick, and she possessed tact — that quality most necessary to social intercourse, but which cannot be taught to those who have it not.

Her reception by the society to which she now belonged, was better than she expected; and though she had to bear some scorn and contumely from the higher-born, she made some real and true friends, and was much admired by the gentlemen. Her beauty was now a disadvantage, for it made the women envious and jealous, and the men gallant and flattering. She was bright and lively in conversation, clever at keeping up a joke, and quick at repartee, so her society was very much courted by the officers of her husband's regiment. The surgeon, especially, as having more leisure, was her constant guest, and used to read to her from the best authors, and explain to her what her very limited education made unintelligible. This is what her husband should have done, but he was idle and careless, and preferred playing billiards, or cards, with his comrades.

She spoke to me once of this period of her life as full of danger. She had become an object of strong interest and affection to a refined and cultivated man. She was grateful to him for improving and elevating her intellect, and for a thousand kind attentions, such as her thoughtless young husband never paid her. She wished to regard him as a brother, and treated him as such; but he put more of the lover into his manner and conversation than she thought proper. She tried to keep her husband more at home, but in vain. At last she told him in a joking way that if he was not more attentive to her, she should fall in love with the doctor, who was so devoted to her. Her husband laughed, and said he would trust her. That expression helped her. Happily she had read none of those bad novels which undermine the morals of the present day. She never heard of the doctrine of affinities; she had read her Bible, and believed in its strictest requirements, and made up her mind to deny herself the society of one who might become too dear to her. Her dangerous friend was obliged to be absent from his regiment for several weeks. There was one particular color which she sometimes wore, and which he disliked so much that he begged her never to wear it; and in a last chat with her before his departure, he said, "If I should see you with that color on when I return, I shall think that you no longer care anything about me."

On that speech she acted,—was arrayed in the obnoxious color on the evening of his return, and met him in the rooms of a friend, not in her own.

The intimacy was broken off and never renewed. He felt it so much that he could not bear to be near her and not with her, so he exchanged into another regiment and never saw her more.

A fit of illness made her husband dependent on her ministrations and brought them again into close communion with each other. It also gave a serious turn to his mind, and he rose up from that sickness a better and a wiser man.

Several years after, when peace was made with France, and the militia was disbanded, he determined to enter the Church, and began his studies accordingly. It was at this time that I first knew him and his charming wife. They hired one of my father's cottages, and became very intimate in our family. We lived in the diocese of the Bishop of St. David's; and he refused to ordain men who, having left a military life, wished to become clergymen, because he thought they did it merely as a means of support, without any fitness for the vocation. The Bishop of Sodor and Man had no such scruples; so Mr. B—— went to the Isle of Man, and having resided there six months, was ordained. About the same time a relation died to whom he was heir-at-law, and he came into possession of a handsome estate in Devonshire; and for the sake of performing his part as a clergyman, he became curate to an absent rector, and did duty in the parish church near his residence. His wife graced her new position, and her cup of happiness was made full to the brim by becoming the mother of a fine boy.

CHAPTER XXXVIII.

LUNATIC ASYLUMS.

IT has always been the custom for meritorious deeds of arms to be rewarded by titles and honors, but it is only in modern times that peaceful civilians have been so rewarded for services rendered to their fellow-citizens. A signal instance of this occurs to me in the case of a physician, who, for his humane treatment of insane patients, was knighted by Queen Victoria. I refer to Sir William Ellis. He was at the head of the great lunatic asylum for paupers at Hanwell, near London, which I once visited, and saw the happy effects of his system on eight hundred patients, who were there taken care of without coercion or severity of any kind. No strait-waistcoats, no strapping patients into beds or chairs, no punishments of any kind were used,—nothing but the personal influence of Sir William and Lady Ellis; and their power over all under their care was extraordinary. Even persons in the height of an attack of mania yielded to it. Part of their system was to keep the patients as fully and as happily employed as was possible, and the whole establishment was like a great school of industry. The pleasure-grounds and the gardens were all kept in order by the patients, watched over by competent persons. Sir William Ellis took great pains to imbue with his own spirit of kindness and patience all whom he employed in the care of the insane, and Lady Ellis was a true helpmate to him.

The extraordinary success of the mild treatment in the Hanwell Asylum soon became known, and numerous applications for admittance there were made by the rich and great, who would pay any price to secure such treatment for their insane relations; but their ability to pay was a complete bar to their reception, — none but the very poor could be received at Hanwell.

The number of paying patients thus refused admittance to the pauper asylum was so great, that it put it into the heads of some philanthropists to establish an asylum for the rich, on the same plan as that at Hanwell, but with such accommodations as would be in accordance with the manner of living to which the wealthy were accustomed. A handsome country-seat was hired, within twenty miles of London, a physician chosen to preside over it, with a fixed salary, and an educated person employed to take care of each insane patient. Carriages and horses were provided for their use, and a row-boat, on a piece of water made to look like a river, was a never-failing source of amusement. A billiard-table too was a great resource in wet weather. Every evening a spacious and handsome drawing-room was well lighted, and the patients, attendants, the physician and his wife, with any guests who happened to be there, would assemble in it and amuse themselves with various games, music, and conversation, till nine o'clock, when family prayers were attended in a pretty chapel in the house, after which all retired for the night.

When I visited this invalid establishment, as it was called, there were about a dozen patients in it who were not very insane, and nearly as many educated attendants. Some of these were well-bred persons, who dined at the same table with the patients and guests; and a stranger, dining with them, could not distinguish the sane from the insane, so well did the patients behave themselves. One of them, an elderly clergyman of the Church of England, always said grace before and after dinner. He was quite a character, and amused the whole household with his sallies of wit, his poetic effusions, and his various peculiarities. One fine morning there was an unusual flocking of patients and guests to the river, where this reverend gentleman had decorated the boat with boughs of trees and red bandanna handkerchiefs. He called it Cleopatra's barge, and was handing in an old lady of seventy to give her a row in it. Some of the visitors had tried to frighten her from going on the water with an insane man; but she knew no fear, and when he invited her into Cleopatra's barge, she delighted him by saying, "If I am Cleopatra, you must be Mark Antony." When she had been out long enough and wished to land, he was not willing to go back until she reminded him that Mark Antony always did exactly as Cleopatra wished. That was sufficient to make him return immediately. The same brave old lady was visiting a patient who was confined to her room, for a few days, because she could not command herself sufficiently well to be in the drawing-room. The attendant who had been sitting with her asked the visitor if she was willing to remain there while she went down to her dinner. She assented, and was locked into the room with the refractory patient. They were seated on each side of the fireplace, when the invalid said, "Are you not afraid to be left with me when that poker is so near me?" "Oh! no," replied the old lady, "not while I have the tongs and shovel so near me.". The patient laughed, and was very quiet and inoffensive.

I have mentioned guests as being in this institution, because the friends of the patients were allowed to visit them occasionally, when deemed proper by the physician of the establishment.

In strong contrast with the instances I have given of persons not at all afraid of the insane, is one which I remember of unreasonable alarm. Among the companions of my girlhood was one, remarkably pretty and amiable, but always laughed at for being a great coward. She had many admirers, and was early married to an excellent youth with a good fortune. She became mistress of one of those charming country-seats, for which England is so remarkable, and enjoyed for a short time the happiness of a true union. Soon, however, her husband showed great uneasiness of mind, and when driving out with his wife, expressed fears of being waylaid, and avoided passing through woods lest his enemies should start out from behind trees. This of course frightened her almost out of her wits, and she became very miserable. A brother of hers paid her a visit, was told of her fears and alarms, and assured her there was no cause for them. He saw at once that his brother-in-law was insane and needed care. The next morning, while the young wife was making her tea on the breakfast-table, and her husband was standing opposite to her, she saw two men enter softly behind him, take hold of his arms and lead him off. She screamed and fell on the floor in a swoon. Her brother was at hand to soothe and comfort her with the assurance that her husband was not seized by his enemies, as she supposed, but by those who would take the best care of him.

By degrees he informed her that her husband was insane and needed restraint; but that in all probability the malady would be only temporary. As soon as she was convinced that he was deranged, she was reconciled to the separation, and thanked her brother for it. Her fear of the insane was so extreme that she never could be persuaded to see her husband again, though he recovered his health, and lived several years a sane but almost broken-hearted man. He corresponded with his wife, and her letters betrayed such a dread of meeting him, that to allay her fears and make her life more tranquil, he went abroad to live, and promised her never to set foot in England. Even this great proof of his generous affection could not overcome her unreasonable fears. They never met again.

After being a widow several years, she made another very happy match, lived without any alarms for one year, became a mother, and lost her reason for life.

One of the most interesting varieties in cases of derangement is that in which the patient ascribes mind and meaning to all inanimate objects. I remember an interesting case of this kind in

England. Some friends of mine were assembled round the door of a charity school, waiting for the arrival of a committee, who were to distribute the prizes, when a very singular-looking old man attracted their attention. In those days the hair and beard were usually cut short; his had not been shorn for years; his hair lay in rolls about his shoulders, and his beard, which was quite white and silvery, concealed all his face below the nose; it appeared to be arranged with great care, as Rubens used to paint beards. From the midst of so much white hair his sparkling eyes and hooked nose looked out like those of an owl, yet the eyes were full of happiness, and sparkled with joy, not fierceness. His dress seemed to be new, and consisted of an olive-colored, square-cut coat, a dark blue waistcoat of the oldest fashion, a pair of yellow velveteen breeches, which were loose enough to form fine draperies, and blue stockings. He was very upright, and moved with an abrupt and nimble air. He stood apart and eyed the company with piercing and inquisitive glances, when one who knew him thus addressed him: "Why, Fitz-Hugh, how is it I see you with a *black* hat on?" "It is not my choice, you may be sure." "What is your objection to black?" "Why you know all colors are but emblems, and black is an emblem of faith falsified. O, it is a shocking color!" "Then what would you wear for mourning?" "An autumn tint, to be sure; autumn is mourning." "Are you still favored to discern spirits as you used to be?" said some one. "Yes," said he, with a most happy and satisfied smile; "O yes! at this moment I see a *spirit of fairness* on that young man," pointing to a well-dressed stranger, who had drawn near to hear what was saying, but drew back abashed, as every one involuntarily turned to look for the *spirit of fairness.*

Fitz-Hugh used to be seen *walking triangles* on the Common, or staring like an eagle at the sun, *waiting for a sign.* He was very religious, and continually whispered to himself, "Peace, peace," in the most emphatic way.

I used to wish that Sir Walter Scott had known this charming old man, he would have figured so well in one of his tales.

CHAPTER XXXIX.

COURTS OF LAW.

I ALWAYS admired Sir Francis Burdett for avoiding the ovation prepared for him by the common people, on his release from the Tower, where he had been confined for a political offence. He feared that the zeal of his friends and admirers might lead them into difficulty, and he had too much regard for them to expose them to danger on his account; so, with a truly generous self-denial, he declined all the honors intended for him, and quietly left the Tower, in a boat, while the streets were crowded for miles with people waiting to welcome him. His enemies called this a cowardly act; but I was among his friends, and heard it spoken of as a noble instance of his humanity.

Many years afterwards, I was visiting in Surrey, England, when Sir Francis Burdett was tried there for *breach of prison*, and being the guest of a family who were radical in their politics, and admirers of Sir Francis, we all went to the court-house in Guildford to hear the trial. He had been imprisoned again, for what offence I cannot remember, and wishing to use his personal influence, in some cause of human liberty, he had escaped from confinement; but having served his purpose, he suffered himself to be recaptured, and returned to prison. He escaped by pretending to change his sofa for a better one, and was carried out concealed in the bed of the rejected sofa. For this breach of prison he was now to be tried at the Guildford assize court. The trial was scarcely begun before it was very evident that the bench and the bar were very hostile to him; but the common people, who thronged the court-room, considered him their champion, and listened to the proceedings with very friendly interest.

Sir Francis refused to employ counsel; he chose to plead his own cause, and did it with dignity and composure. His appearance was that of a man between forty and fifty years of age, in delicate health, but full of mental vigor. His plea was, that he had not broken any law; he said the very meaning of imprisonment was keeping a man shut up against his will, and if any one was guilty it was the jailer, for suffering him to escape. He stated this so clearly and forcibly that it made the trial seem to be a ridiculous farce. In the course of his speech, he took occasion to broach many of his radical opinions, and to give severe cuts at many old abuses;

he was often called to order by the judge and the lawyers, who became highly irritated as he proceeded. Though often interrupted, he managed to say much that he wished the people to hear, made a very capital defence of his *breach of prison*, and was, I believe, let off with a small fine and costs.

I was once in an English court when a man was tried for stealing a sheep, and death was at that time the penalty, if proved guilty. I listened to the evidence with the painful assurance that it must convict him; but in spite of it, and of the judge's charge being dead against the prisoner, the jury brought in a verdict of "not guilty," owing, no doubt, to their horror of taking life for the theft of a sheep.

My next experience of courts was in Newport, Rhode Island, where Judge Story took me to his circuit court, on purpose to hear Daniel Webster plead against a man who had taken charge of a large sum of money, in doubloons, to oblige a friend, and had been robbed of them. The plea for the defence was very able and seemed unanswerable; but when Mr. Webster spoke, he tore in rags and tatters the web of reasoning which had just appeared so strong, and made one feel ashamed of having supposed the man who lost the money could be excused for it. The court rang with the deep sonorous voice of Mr. Webster, when he pronounced the words "unpardonable negligence" again and again, in the most emphatic tones. He won the case and won the admiration of all who heard him. Mr. Webster was then in his prime, and he looked the grand character that he was. Judge Story, too, was the *beau ideal* of a judge. His serene and benevolent countenance gave the promise of as much mercy as was compatible with justice. I happened to be at Newport when the Circuit Court was sitting there and saw much of those two great men, and the impression they made on me at that time was so strong, that in writing this, I seem to see them before me and hear again their voices, though it is more than forty years ago.

I never was again in an American court of law, until a few years since, when I went from Baltimore to Washington, on purpose to hear Jacob Barker plead his own cause before the judges of the Supreme Court, who listened to him with evident pleasure for four consecutive days, and for three or four hours each day.

His claim on the United States government dated back to the time of the war with England in 1812. At that period of great financial distress in the treasury department, Jacob Barker raised a large loan for the government, and this has never been fully repaid, though he has been prosecuting his claim ever since. In stating his case before the judges, he gave an interesting and very spirited review of the whole period, interspersed with lively anecdotes, and delivered with great energy and fluency.

The first day of his speaking the Attorney-General was present, and after listening for an hour, he tried to stop Mr. Barker, and begged the judges not to let him go on at such length. But they said they would listen to Mr. Barker as long as he pleased to speak; on which the Attorney-General left the court, and never appeared again till Mr. Barker had finished. This long plea was made by an octogenarian, and no young man could have done it with more energy, acuteness, or vivacity.

CHAPTER XL.

MISS DELIA BACON.

THE first lady whom I ever heard deliver a public lecture was Miss Delia Bacon, who opened her career in Boston, as teacher of history, by giving a preliminary discourse, describing her method, and urging upon her hearers the importance of the study.

I had called on her that day for the first time, and found her very nervous and anxious about her first appearance in public. She interested me at once, and I resolved to hear her speak. Her person was tall and commanding, her finely shaped head was well set on her shoulders, her face was handsome and full of expression, and she moved with grace and dignity. The hall in which she spoke was so crowded that I could not get a seat, but she spoke so well that I felt no fatigue from standing. She was at first a little embarrassed, but soon became so engaged in recommending the study of history to all present, that she ceased to think of herself, and then she became eloquent.

Her course of oral lessons, or lectures, on history interested her class of ladies so much that she was induced to repeat them, and I heard several who attended them speak in the highest terms of them. She not only spoke, but read well, and when on the subject of Roman history, she delighted her audience by giving them with great effect some of Macaulay's Lays.

I persuaded her to give her lessons in Cambridge, and she had a very appreciative class assembled in the large parlor of the Brattle House. She spoke without notes, entirely from her own well-stored memory; and she would so group her facts as to present to us historical pictures calculated to make a lasting impression. She was so much admired and liked in Cambridge, that a lady there invited her to spend the winter with her as her guest, and I gave her the use of my parlor for another course of lectures. In these she brought down her history to the time of the birth of Christ, and I can never forget how clear she made it to us that the world was only then made fit for the advent of Jesus. She ended with a fine climax that was quite thrilling.

In her Cambridge course she had maps, charts, models, pictures, and everything she needed to illustrate her subject. This added much to her pleasure and ours. All who saw her then must remember how handsome she was, and how gracefully she used her wand in pointing to the illustrations of her subject. I used to be reminded by her of Raphael's sibyls, and she often spoke like an oracle.

She and a few of her class would often stay after the lesson and take tea with me, and then she would talk delightfully for the rest of the evening. It was very inconsiderate in us to allow her to do so, and when her course ended she was half dead with fatigue. She expressed a great desire to go to England, and I told her she could go and pay all her expenses by her historical lessons. Belonging to a religious sect in which her family held a distinguished place, she would be well received by the same denomination in England, and have the best of assistance in obtaining classes. After talking this up for some time, I perceived that I was talking in vain. She had no notion of going to England to teach history; all she wanted to go for was to obtain proof of the truth of her theory, that Shakespeare did not write the plays attributed to him, but that Lord Bacon did. This was sufficient to prevent my ever again encouraging her going to England, or talking with her about Shakespeare. The lady whom she was visiting put her copy of his works out of sight, and never allowed her to converse with her on this, her favorite subject. We considered it dangerous for Miss Bacon to dwell on this fancy, and thought that, if indulged, it might become a monomania, which it subsequently did.

She went from Cambridge to Northampton, and spent the summer on Round Hill, as a boarder at a hydropathic establishment. Separated from all who knew her, and were interested in her, she gave herself up to her favorite theme. She believed that the plays called Shakespeare's contained a double meaning, and that a whole system of philosophy was hidden in them, which the world at that time was not prepared to receive, and therefore Lord Bacon had left it to posterity thus disguised. At Round Hill she spent whole days and weeks in her chamber, took no exercise, and ate scarcely any food, till she became seriously ill. After much suffering she recovered and went to New York. To pay her expenses she was obliged to give a course of lessons on history; but her heart was not in them, — she was meditating a flight to England. Her old friends and her relations would not of course furnish her with the means of doing what they highly disapproved; but some new acquaintances in New York believed in her theory, and were but too happy to aid her in making known her grand discovery. A handsome wardrobe and ample means were freely bestowed upon her, and kind friends attended her to the vessel which was to carry her to England on her Quixotic expedition. Her mind was so devoted to the genius of Lord Bacon that her first pilgrimage was to St. Albans, where he had lived when in retirement, and where she supposed that he had written all those plays attributed to Shakespeare. She lived there a year, and then came to London, all alone and unknown, to seek a home there. She thus describes her search after lodgings: "On a dark December day, about one o'clock, I came into this metropolis, intending, with the aid of Providence, to select, between that and nightfall, a residence in it. I had copied from the Times several advertisements of lodging-houses, but none of them suited me. The cab-driver, perceiving what I was in search of, began to make suggestions of his own, and finding that he was a man equal to the emergency, and knowing that his acquaintance with the subject was larger than mine, I put the business into his hands. I told him to stop at the first good house which he thought would suit me, and he brought me to this door, where I have been ever since. Any one who thinks this is not equal to Elijah and his raven, and Daniel in the lions' den, does not know what it is for a lady, and a stranger, to live for a year in London, without any money to speak of, maintaining all the time the position of a lady, and a distinguished lady too; and above all, such a one cannot be acquainted with the nature of cab-drivers and lodging-house keepers in general. The one with whom I lodge has behaved to me like an absolute gentleman. No one could have shown more courtesy and delicacy. For six months at a time he has never sent me a bill; before this I had always paid him weekly, and I believe that is customary. When after waiting six months I sent him ten pounds, and he knew that it was all I had, he wrote a note to me, which I preserve as a curiosity, to say that he would entirely prefer that I should keep it. I have lived upon this man's confidence in me for a year, and this comparatively pleasant and comfortable home is one that I owe to the judgment and taste of a cab-driver. . . . . Your ten pounds was brought me two or three hours after your letter came, and I sent it immediately to Mr. Walker, and now I am entirely relieved of that most painful feeling of the impropriety of depending upon him in this way, which it has required all my faith and philosophy to endure, because he can now very well wait for the rest, and perceive that the postponement is not an indefinite one. Your letter has warmed my heart, and that was what had suffered most. I would have frozen into a Niobe before I would have asked any help for myself, and would sell gingerbread and apples at the corner of a street for the rest of my days before I could stoop, for myself, to such humiliations as I have borne in behalf of my work, which was the world's work, and I knew that I had a right to demand aid for it."

In her first interview with Carlyle she told him of her great discovery in regard to Shakespeare's plays, so called, and he appeared to be interested in her, if not in her hypothesis; but he treated that with respect, and advised her to put her thoughts on paper. She accordingly accepted an arrangement, kindly made for her by Mr. R. W. Emerson with the editors of a Boston magazine, worked very hard, and soon sent off eighty pages. A part of this was published, and she received eighteen pounds for it. Had this contract been carried out, the money made by it would have supported her comfortably in London, but there arose some misunderstanding between her and the editors, owing, perhaps, to her want of method and ignorance of business. She considered herself very ill-used, and would have nothing more to do with them. Her theory should be set forth in a book.

She now found an excellent and powerful friend in Mr. Hawthorne. He kindly undertook to make an agreement with a publisher, and promised her that her book should be printed if she would write it. Deprived of her expected emolument from writing articles for a periodical, she was much distressed for want of funds, and suffered many privations during the time that she was writing her book. She lived on the poorest food, and was often without the means of having a fire in her chamber. She told me that she wrote a great part of her large octavo volume sitting up in bed, in order to keep warm.

It was when her work was about half done that she wrote to me the letter from which I have made the foregoing extract. Her life of privation and seclusion was very injurious to both body and mind. How great that seclusion was, is seen in the following passage from another of her letters to me.

"I am glad to know that you are still alive and on this side of that wide sea which parts me from so many that were once so *near*, for I have lived here much like a departed spirit, looking back on the joys and sorrows of a world in which I have no longer any place. I have been more than a year in this house, and have had but three visitors in all that time, and paid but one visit myself, and that was to Carlyle, after he had taken the trouble to come all the way from Chelsea to invite me, and though he has since written to invite me, I have not been able to accept his kindness. I have had calls from Mr. Grote and Mr. Monckton Milnes; and Mr. Buchanan came to see me, though I had not delivered my letter to him."

All the fine spirits who knew Miss Bacon found

in her what pleased and interested them, and had not that one engrossing idea possessed her, she might have had a brilliant career among the literary society of London.

One dark winter evening, after writing all day in her bed, she rose, threw on some clothes, and walked out to take the air. Her lodgings were at the West End of London, near to Sussex Gardens, and not far from where my mother lived. She needed my address, and suddenly resolved to go to the house of Mrs. R—— for it. She sent in her request, and while standing in the doorway she had a glimpse of the interior. It looked warm, cheerful, and inviting, and she had a strong desire to see my mother; so she readily accepted an invitation to walk in, and found the old lady with her daughter and a friend just sitting down to tea. Happily my sister remembered that a Miss Bacon had been favorably mentioned in my letters from Cambridge, so she had no hesitation in asking her to take tea with them. The stranger's dress was such an extraordinary *dishabille* that nothing but her ladylike manners and conversation could have convinced the family that she was the person whom she pretended to be. She told me how much ashamed she was of her appearance that evening; she had intended going only to the door, but could not resist the inclination to enter and sit down at that cheerful teatable, which looked so like mine in Cambridge.

The next summer I was living in London. The death of a dear friend had just occurred in my house; the relatives were collected there, and all were feeling very sad, when I was told by my servant that a lady wished to see me. I sent word that there was death in the house and I could see no one that night. The servant returned, saying, "She will not go away, ma'am, and she will not give her name."

On hearing this I went to the door, and there stood Delia Bacon, pale and sad. I took her in my arms and pressed her to my bosom; she gasped for breath and could not speak. We went into a vacant room and sat down together. She was faint, but recovered on drinking a glass of port wine, and then she told me that her book was finished and in the hands of Mr. Hawthorne, and now she was ready to go to Stratford-upon-Avon. There she expected to verify her hypothesis, by opening the tomb of Shakespeare, where she felt sure of finding papers that would disclose the real authorship of the plays. I tried in vain to dissuade her from this insane project; she was resolved, and only wished for my aid in winding up her affairs in London and setting her off for Stratford. This aid I gave with many a sad misgiving as to the result. She looked so ill when I took leave of her in the railroad carriage that I blamed myself for not having accompanied her to Stratford, and was only put at ease by a very cheerful letter from her, received a few days after her departure.

On arriving at Stratford she was so exhausted that she could only creep up to bed at the inn, and when she inquired about lodgings it was doubtful to herself, and all who saw her, whether she would live to need any. One person expressed this to her, but her brave heart and strong will carried her out the next day in search of a home, and here as in London she fell into good hands. She entered a very pretty cottage, the door of which stood open, found no one in it, but sat down and waited for some one to appear. Presently the owner entered, an elderly lady, living on her income, with only one servant. She had never taken any lodger, but she would not send Miss Bacon away, because she was a stranger and ill; and she remembered, she said, that Abraham had entertained angels unawares. So she made her lie down on her sofa, and covered her up, and went off to prepare some dinner for her. Miss Bacon says, in her letter to me: "There I was, at the same hour when I left you, the day before, looking out upon the trees that skirt the Avon, and that church and spire only a few yards from me, but so weak that I did not expect ever to go there. I know that I have been very near death. If anything can restore me it will be the motherly treatment I have here."

A few weeks after this, I received a very cheerful letter from her on the subject of the publisher of her book. She writes, "I want you to help me; help me bear this new kink of burden which I am so little used to. The editor of Fraser's Magazine, Parker, the very best publisher in England, is going to publish my book immediately, in such haste that they cannot stay to send me the proofs. That was the piece of news which came with your letter. How I wished it had been yourself instead, that you might share it with me on the instant. It was a relief to me to be assured that your generous heart was so near to be gladdened with it. Patience has had its perfect work. For the sake of those who have loved and trusted me, for the sake of those who have borne my burdens with me, how I rejoice!

"Mr. Bennock writes to me for the title, and says this has been suggested, 'The Shakespeare Problem Solved by Delia Bacon'; but I am afraid that, with the name, sounds too boastful. I have thought of suggesting 'The Shakespeare Problem, by Delia Bacon,' leaving the reader to infer the rest. I have also thought of calling it 'The Baconian Philosophy in Prose and Verse, by Delia Bacon'; or the 'Fables of the Baconian Philosophy.' But the publishers are the best judges of such things."

That the book should be published under such agreeable auspices was the crowning blessing of her arduous labors, and it is a comfort to her friends that this gleam of sunshine illumined her path before the clouds settled down more darkly than ever on her fine mind.

She remained for several months in Stratford, but I believe she never attempted to open the tomb of Shakespeare; and when she left that place, she returned home to die in the bosom of her family. Thus ends the history of a highly gifted and noble-minded woman.

THE END.

Cambridge : Stereotyped and Printed by Welch, Bigelow, & Co.

www.ingramcontent.com/pod-product-compliance
Lightning Source LLC
LaVergne TN
LVHW020211110826
845151LV00003B/679

* 9 7 8 1 4 2 5 5 3 4 6 4 6 *